Pra

'A remarkable engagement between a philosopher and
a poet . . . written both with a beautiful, poised
lucidity and calm, candid passion.'
Steven Connor, Birkbeck College, London

'Critchley writes with brilliant wit, clarity, penetration, and
a disarming modesty . . . Altogether it is a terrific book.'
J. Hillis Miller, University of California, Irvine

'Characteristically engaging and stimulating,
clear and succinct.'
Sebastian Gardner, University College London

PP. 3°··,ꢀ (Ȉ₂ᵢ")

Things Merely Are

This book is an invitation to read poetry. Simon Critchley argues that poetry enlarges life with a range of observation, power of expression and attention to language that eclipses any other medium. In an extended engagement with the poetry of Wallace Stevens, Critchley reveals that poetry also contains deep and important philosophical insight. Above all, he argues for a 'poetic epistemology' that enables us to recast the philosophical problem of the relation between mind and world, or thought and things, in a way that allows us to cast the problem away.

Drawing on Kant, the German and English Romantics and Heidegger, Critchley argues that, through its descriptions of particular things and their difficult plainness, poetry evokes the 'mereness' of things. Poetry brings us to the realization that things merely are, an experience that provokes a mood of calm, a calm that allows the imagination to press back against the pressure of reality. Critchley also argues that this calm defines the cinematic eye of Terrence Malick, whose work is discussed at the end of the book.

SIMON CRITCHLEY is Professor of Philosophy at the New School for Social Research, New York, and at the University of Essex. He is the author of many books, including *Very Little . . . Almost Nothing* (revised edition, 2004) and *On Humour* (2002), both published by Routledge.

Things Merely Are

Philosophy in the poetry of
Wallace Stevens

Simon Critchley

Routledge
Taylor & Francis Group

LONDON AND NEW YORK

First published 2005
by Routledge
2 Park Square, Milton Park, Abingdon, Oxon OX14 4RN

Simultaneously published in the USA and Canada
by Routledge
270 Madison Ave, New York, NY 10016

Transferred to Digital Printing 2008

Routledge is an imprint of the Taylor & Francis Group, an informa business

© 2005 Simon Critchley

Typeset in Centaur MT by The Running Head Limited, Cambridge
Printed and bound in Great Britain by TJI Digital, Padstow, Cornwall

British Library Cataloguing in Publication Data
A catalogue record for this book is available from the British Library

Library of Congress Cataloging in Publication Data
Critchley, Simon, 1960–
Things merely are: philosophy in the poetry of
Wallace Stevens / Simon Critchley.— 1st ed.
p. cm.
Includes bibliographical references.
1. Stevens, Wallace, 1879–1955—Philosophy. 2. Philosophy in literature.
3. Poetry. I. Title.
PS3537.T4753Z6244 2005
811'.52—dc22
2004014913

ISBN 10: 0-415-35630-X (hbk)
ISBN 10: 0-415-35631-8 (pbk)

ISBN 13: 978-0-415-35630-5 (hbk)
ISBN 13: 978-0-415-35631-2 (pbk)

'To say more than human things with human voice,
That cannot be; to say human things with more
Than human voice, that, also, cannot be;
To speak humanly from the height or from the depth
Of human things, that is acutest speech.'

Wallace Stevens, 'Chocorua to its Neighbor'

Contents

Acknowledgements

The author and publisher wish to thank Faber & Faber and Random House, USA, for kind permission to reprint the following poems by Wallace Stevens: 'Of Modern Poetry', 'The American Sublime', 'Song of a Fixed Accord', 'The Dove in Spring', 'The Course of a Particular', 'Of Mere Being', 'First Warmth', 'As You Leave the Room' and 'The Death of a Soldier'.

Abbreviations of works by Wallace Stevens

.

PM – *The Palm at the End of the Mind,* edited by Holly Stevens (Vintage, New York, 1967)

NA – *The Necessary Angel. Essays on Reality and the Imagination* (Knopf, New York, 1951/Faber, London, 1960)

CP – *Collected Poems* (Knopf, New York, 1955/Faber, London, 1955)

OP – *Opus Posthumous,* revised, enlarged and corrected edition, edited by Milton J. Bates (Knopf, New York, 1989/Faber, London, 1990)

Advice to the reader

I do not write poetry. T.S. Eliot writes somewhere that the only poets to be taken seriously are those who write after the age of twenty-five. I stopped writing poetry a few months after my twenty-fifth birthday. I used to write delicately crafted little observations of architecture, landscape and other usually inert things, all wrapped up in obscure verse forms, the more obscure the better (I never did finish my sestina, but wrote a few middling villanelles). Like so many of my generation, I had come to the experience of poetry through reading T.S. Eliot, first the early verse like 'The Wasteland' and then increasingly the later work like 'Four Quartets'. Dimly echoing this movement, I had gone from a bad Nietzschean free-versifying doggerel of confessional fragments, to a sub-Eliotesque obsession with form, with metre, rhyme, stanzas and the whole realm of the wrought. Sadly, as my cultivation of form developed, I seemed to have less and less to say. Almost nothing, in fact. Then, when I was around twenty-four, I read W.H. Auden, a poet whom I had deliberately avoided until then for reasons that now escape me. Now, Auden had lots of things to say and could say them in seemingly any form he chose. Furthermore, he did not seem to find writing poetry terribly difficult. I did. So, I wrote a poem about Auden, about how good he was, and that was my last poem. I devoted the next years of writing to philosophy and became a reader of poetry. This was how I discovered Wallace Stevens, amongst others.

The point of this autobiographical anecdote is to underline what I think is going on in the following pages: it is an invitation to read poetry. If I have a general cultural complaint it is that, first and most importantly, there are too few readers of poetry and, second but relatedly, too many of those readers are writers of poetry. It is the general conviction of this book that poetry elevates, liberates and ennobles human life and that the experience of poetry should be extended to as many people as possible. Poetry enlarges life with a range of observation, a depth of sentiment, a power of expression and an attention to language that simply eclipses any other medium. As I say below, poetry is life with the ray of imagination's power shot through it. It is my belief that a life without poetry is a life diminished, needlessly stunted. Yet, I also know, from colleagues in schools and literature departments, that poetry is enormously difficult to teach and is often much less popular than the teaching of novels or drama, let alone film or television. The *idée fixe* that needs to be unfixed is that poetry is difficult and therefore to be avoided. Yes, poetry *is* difficult and that's why it shouldn't be avoided. The difficulty is learning to love that difficulty, becoming accustomed to the experience of thinking that poetry requires and calls forth. Eliot writes somewhere else that poetry should communicate before it is understood, which is precisely right. The difficulty of reading poetry is acquiring the patience and allowing the time for communication to become understanding.

The following pages offer an invitation to read poetry by focusing on the work of one poet, Wallace Stevens, and trying to show how his verse exemplifies what poetry is capable of when mind and language are working together at full stretch. Without wanting to diminish the man, it is fair to say that Stevens's life was not lived at full stretch. This has the great merit of deflecting attention away from the reductive obsession with biography that dominates discussion of much literature, and focusing on Stevens's words. Wallace Stevens was born in Reading, Pennsylvania, in 1879 and died in Hartford, Connecticut, in 1955. He gained late recognition for his poetry and his first collection, *Harmonium*, was published in 1923 when Stevens was in his forty-fourth year. His next collection, *Ideas of Order*, appeared thirteen years later in 1936 and was followed by several others, culminating in the publication of *The Collected Poems* in 1955, for which he won the Pulitzer Prize for Poetry and his second National Book Award in Poetry. A further, fuller, 1967 edition of Stevens's work, which importantly includes some of the late poems not included in *The Collected Poems* appeared as *The Palm at the End of the Mind*, edited by his daughter, Holly Stevens. Stevens was a lawyer and from 1916 onwards he was associated with Hartford Accident and Indemnity Company, where he worked on its fidelity and surety claims. He even wrote a couple of short papers on insurance that can be found together with many much more interesting things in the *Opus Posthumous* that appeared in 1959 and in an extended second

3

edition in 1989. He became a vice-president of the company in 1934, but refused all corporate advancement after that date. He was both proud of his work and seemingly very good at it. So much for Stevens's life.

I teach philosophy for a living and my angle of entry into Stevens is philosophical, but this should suggest nothing intimidating or parochial. I think Stevens's poetry allows us to recast what is arguably the fundamental concern of philosophy, namely the relation between thought and things or mind and world, the concern that becomes, in the early modern period, the basic problem of epistemology. It will be my general claim that Stevens recasts this concern in a way that lets us cast it away. Stevens's verse shows us a way of over-coming epistemology. Therefore, and this is important to my overall approach, I am not mining Stevens's verse for philosophical puzzles and *aperçus* in pleasing poetic garb. Nothing would be more fatuous. On the contrary, I am trying to show two things: first, that Stevens's poetry – and by implication much other poetry – contains deep, consequent and instructive philosophical insight, and second that this insight is best expressed poetically. It is not, therefore, a question of paraphrasing obscure poetic rumination in clear philosophical prose, but rather of trying to point towards an experience of mind, language and things that is best articulated in poetic form. I am painfully aware of the fact that this entire enterprise is a performa-tive self-contradiction, but see no other option, short of writing poetry myself, which I will spare you for reasons already given. Many of you will have heard of the ancient quarrel between philosophy and poetry that begins in Plato's *Republic*, itself a dramatic dialogue, and is one of the dominant and ever-twisting storylines in sub-

advice to the reader

sequent Western history. This book is not an attempt to settle that quarrel, but rather a call for the disputing parties to see the terms of the quarrel in a fresh light. I very much hope that it will set new quarrels in motion.

What I find in Stevens, what I see his verse moving towards, is a meditative voice, a voice that is not shrill, but soft yet tenacious. This voice speaks of things, of things both in their unexceptional plainness and their peculiar gaudiness. It also speaks of itself, of the activity of mind and imagination that make up a self, a self that comes to find itself in relation to things. What I hope to communicate to the reader is some experience of this voice, of its grain and goal. Although scholars who know Stevens's verse much better than I might disagree, I think this voice is at its most compelling in Stevens's late poems. These are the topic of chapter 6, although I make my way towards them in the preceding chapters. In sharp distinction from the florid and Floridian landscape of the earlier poems, the habitat of Stevens's late poetry is exceptionally minimal; it is composed of pond, leaves, trees, the sun and moon, and the occasional animal, usually a bird, sometimes a rat. Its season, in Stevens's symbolic calendar, is not the imaginative flowering of summer or the hard reality of winter, but the in-between times of early spring and late winter. If there is a mood to Stevens's late poetry it is an experience of calm, the calm that comes from learning to look at things, being there with things in a way that does not seek to dominate them or appropriate them to the understanding. It is Stevens's conviction, whose philosophical ancestry I will try to unearth, that things are what they are through an act of the mind, what he calls the imagination. Thus, it is ultimately through the

5

activity of mind that there is a world for us, a world that appears to be ordered, familiar, coherent and significant. However, although reality is given to us through an act of the mind, Stevens's late poems stubbornly show how the mind cannot seize hold of the ultimate nature of the reality that faces it. Reality retreats before the imagination that shapes and orders it. Poetry is therefore the experience of failure. As Stevens puts it in a famous late poem, the poet gives us ideas about the thing, not the thing itself. The insight towards which I see Stevens's verse making its way is an acceptance of both the necessity of poetry and its limitation, the acknowledgement that things merely are and that we are things too, things endowed with imagination. Far from any otherworldly sophism, in a language free from mysticism, Stevens's poetry can teach a certain disposition of calm, an insight into things that comes from having them in sight. Stevens can teach a thoughtfulness in the face of things and encourage a certain humility and nobility. In the face of overwhelming pressure of a reality defined by the noise of war and ever-enlarging incoherence of information, the cultivation of such a disposition might allow us, in Stevens's words, to press back against that pressure of reality with the power of poetic imagination and keep open the precious space of reflection.

Hopefully, the book will speak for itself and speak to the reader, although he or she might choose to skip some of the slightly neurotic philosophical throat-clearing at the end of chapter 2. Let me also explain two oddities, one at the beginning and the other at the end of the book. First, I begin by trying to communicate the concerns of Stevens's poetry in a rather aphoristic manner which might appear either queer or cute or simply odd. Some of those words are

advice to the reader

mine, some are Stevens's, and some are borrowed from other inter-
locutors. Second, I end the book with a discussion of the movies of
Terrence Malick, whose work has long been a passion of mine. I
find in Malick's movies a set of deeply Stevensian concerns, particularly the difficulty of communicating philosophical thoughts in
cinematic form, of thinking in and on film. What Malick is seeking
to cultivate in his art is a cinematic analogue to Stevens's late poems,
namely an experience of meditation that occurs not through a
retreat from the world, but by relearning to see it in all its quotidian
banality and violent beauty.

New York City
Summer 2004

I

Or so we say — twenty-one propositions

1. Poetry is the description of a particular thing — a tin plate, the loaf of bread on it, the wine that I drink, clear water in a brilliant bowl, a small rock in the palm of my hand, the leafless stubby tree that I see from my kitchen window, the moon in a clear winter's sky.

2. The poet describes those things in the radiant atmosphere produced by the imagination. Poetic acts are thus acts of the mind, which describe recognizable things, real things, *really* real things, but which vary the appearance of those things, changing the aspect under which they are seen. Poetry brings about *felt* variations in the appearance of things. What is most miraculous is that poetry does this simply by the sound of words,

> This city now doth, like a garment, wear
> The beauty of the morning, silent, bare . . .

3. Poetry imaginatively transfigures a common reality, Wordsworth taking a morning walk in London, for example. But that common

reality can press in on the self, the city becomes oppressive and the self depressive. The world becomes a deafening, violent place dominated by an ever-enlarging incoherence of information and the constant presence of war. Such is arguably our present. This is a leaden time, a time of dearth, a world that cannot move for the weight of its own heaviness.

4. What, then, are poets for? In a time of dearth, they resist the pressure of reality, they press back against this oppressiveness with the power of imagination, producing felt variations in the appearance of things. Poetry enables us to feel differently, to see differently. It leavens a leaden time. This is poetry's nobility, which is also a violence, an imaginative violence from within that protects us from the violence from without – violence against violence, then.

5. Poetry is life with the ray of imagination's power passing through it.

6. The poetic act, the act of the mind, illumines the surface of things with imagination's beam. This act is part of the thing and not about it. Through it, we detect what we might call *the movement of the self* in those things: plate, bread, wine, water, rock, tree, moon. In poetry, the makings of things are makings of the self. Poets are the chanting-hearted artificers of the world in which they sing and, singing, make.

7. Words of the world are the life of the world. Or so we say.

8. That which is, is for a self who declares it to be. Philosophically expressed, all poetry is idealistic, at least in ambition. But the *materia poetica*, the raw stuff out of which poetry makes its radiant atmospheres, is the real, real particulars, actual stuff, the incorrigible plurality of things. Poetry is the imagination touching reality.

or could be?

9. Poetry allows us to see things *as* they are. It lets us see particulars being various. But, and this is its peculiarity, poetry lets us see things as they are anew, under a new aspect, transfigured, subject to a felt variation. The poet sings a song that is both beyond us yet ourselves. Things change when the poet sings them, but they are still our things: recognizable, common, near, low. We hear the poet sing and press back against the pressure of reality.

10. It is easily said that the poet makes the ordinary extraordinary. Yet, the extraordinary is only extraordinary if it refers back to the ordinary, otherwise it would be empty. This is another way of drawing the distinction between imagination and fancy: the poetic imagination imagines things as they are, but beyond us, turned about, whereas fancy fantasizes about things that are not: unicorns, gods, golden mountains.

11. We find an order in things. When I look at the boats at anchor in the harbour there, as night descends, their lights tilting in the air, they seem to master the night and portion out the sea, arranging the harbour and fixing the surrounding village. When I place a jar on a hill, the slovenly wilderness that surrounded that hill rises up to that jar and is no longer wild. We find an order in things. Poetry

reorders the order we find in things. It gives us things as they are, but beyond us. Poetry, it might be said, gives us an *idea* of order.

12. Think of truth as troth, as an act of betrothal, of wedding, of pledging oneself to things. *Dichtung und Wahrheit*, poetry and truth, poetry is truthful as trothful. It speaks the truth of things, it speaks the truth out of things, a truth that is both something we recognize and something new, something beyond us yet ourselves.

13. Poetry describes life as it is, but in all the intricate evasions of as. It gives us the world as it is – common, near, low, recognizable – but imagined, illumined, turned about. It is a world both seen and unseen until seen with the poet's eyes.

14. Poetry momentarily focuses the bewilderment to which we are attached and which passes for our inner life.

15. Poetry is an elevation, an enlargement of life. At its noblest, poetry helps people live their lives. At its feeblest, it does not.

16. What is essential is that poetry should produce this elevation, this enlargement, in words free from mysticism, that is, free from any purported intellectual intuition of a transcendent reality. There is no such intuition. I have no reason to believe that there is any such transcendent reality. Poetry might ennoble, but it is acutely mundane.

17. The climate of our world is not perfect. Ours is not the world of gods, monsters and heroes, of the wingèd soul taking flight into

the silent aether, but that of the near, the low, the common, the imperfect. The imperfect is our only paradise. The difficulty is finding paradise in that imperfection.

18. A poet might write poems appropriate to our climate, to the variousness of things scattered around: to cities, towns and villages; to buildings and houses; to birds, plants and trees; to transport systems, the subtleties of trade and the speed of commerce; to weather, heavy weather and slight, to the movement that clouds make over a wet landscape on an afternoon in late November; to a time of war and what passes for peace; to wine, water and the sensation of eating oysters; to air, light and the joy of having a body; to your mother and your lovers, who should not be confused; to the sea: cold, salt, dark, clear, utterly free; to quail, sweet berries and casual flocks of pigeons; to the yellow moon over La Marsa; to your pet cat Jeoffrey who can detect electricity; to the whole voluptuousness of looking.

19. The poet finds words for these things which are not the revelations of religious belief, not the hymns singing of high heaven, but the more precious portents of our powers, of imagination's beam reordering the order we find in the world.

20. If I bang my head on the door, I do not cry out 'Oh God' or 'Sweet warm blood of Jesus', but 'door', 'head' and, most probably, 'ouch'. Poetry can teach this. It is truth, not edification.

21. God is dead, therefore I am. Such is poetry's proposition. Yet, how *is* one? Such is poetry's question.

2

Poetry, philosophy and life as it is

'For we can unsuppose Heaven and Earth and
annihilate the world in our imagination, but
the place where they stood will remain
behind, and we cannot unsuppose or
annihilate that, do what we can.'

Thomas Traherne (1637–74),
Centuries of Meditation II

In my view, Wallace Stevens is the philosophically most interesting
poet to have written in English in the twentieth century. It is
arguable that there are poets as philosophically interesting writing in
languages other than English during this period, and it is also
arguable that there are better poets in English than Stevens. Still, this
is a large claim to make and, in what follows, I would simply like to
persuade you that this is not an entirely preposterous thing to say.
As a philosopher, what it is about Stevens that interests me is the
fact that he found a manner that is wholly poetic, of developing full
thoughts: theses, hypotheses, conjectures, ruminations and apho-
risms that one should call philosophical. As his work developed,
Stevens created a unique meditative form, most often in the late

verse, the blank verse triplet, often grouped into units of six or seven stanzas, as you can see below. Stevens was not prissy or precious about poetic form and what counted for him was freedom of expression, although, of course, this does not imply freedom from form. He wisely writes, 'A free form does not assure freedom' (*OP* 240).

A fine example of this meditative form can be seen in the important long, late poem, 'An Ordinary Evening in New Haven'. This shows Stevens poetically capable not just of stating a proposition, but of initiating a hypothesis – 'if' is a very common word in Stevens's lexicon, 'as if' is even more common, and Stevens's is a philosophy of the 'as if', of what Helen Vendler calls his qualified assertions.[1] He will also suddenly change tack, introducing new personae and topoi, or simply let the poetry slide into comic bathos or very often into sheer sound, into what he variously calls 'the mic-mac of mocking birds' (*PM* 349) or 'the mickey mockers and plated pairs' (*PM* 114). Towards the end of the poem, Stevens writes,

> If it should be true that reality exists
> In the mind: the tin plate, the loaf of bread on it,
> The long-bladed knife, the little to drink and her
>
> Misericordia, it follows that
> Real and unreal are two in one: New Haven
> Before and after one arrives or, say,
>
> Bergamo in a postcard, Rome after dark,
> Sweden described, Salzburg with shaded eyes
> Or Paris in conversation at a café.

poetry, philosophy and life as it is

The endlessly elaborating poem
Displays the theory of poetry,
As the life of poetry. A more severe,

More harassing master would extemporize
Subtler, more urgent proof that the theory
Of poetry is the theory of life,

As it is, in the intricate evasions of as,
In things seen and unseen, created from nothingness,
The heavens, the hells, the worlds, the longed-for lands.

(*PM* 349)

Stevens's language moves from a hypothesis, 'if it is true . . .', to con-crete particulars, 'the tin plate, the loaf of bread on it . . .', to syllogistic conclusions, 'it follows that . . .', to propositions of the most general import, 'the theory of poetry is the theory of life' – with a possible allusion to Coleridge's *Theory of Life*. The proposition is then pursued in the most finely ambiguous manner, where it is a question of life 'as it is, in the intricate evasions of as'. Poetry is ambiguous. This is what appals some philosophers and appeals to others. Poetic language is a matter of what he calls, also from 'An Ordinary Evening',

. . . the edgings and inchings of final form,
The swarming activities of the formulae
Of statement, directly and indirectly getting at . . .

(*PM* 351)

17

Yet, Stevens's qualified assertions, his 'ifs' and 'as ifs', deploy ambiguity to get at the evasiveness of poetry's matter, which is reality,

> We seek
> Nothing beyond reality. Within it,
>
> Everything, the spirit's alchemicana
> Included . . .

(PM 336)

The alchemy here refers, I think, to the transmutation of reality into mind or spirit through the work of thought. But that is not all. Going back to the above passage, we move instantly from grand propositions about the real and unreal into the almost comic, touristic particularity of 'Sweden described, Salzburg with shaded eyes . . .', and from there into moments of visionary lyrical rapture, 'the heavens, the hells, the worlds, the longed-for lands'. The curious and distinctive thing about Stevens, it seems to me, is that all these aspects occur concurrently within the meditative form of the poem: metaphysics, a little casuistry, lyricism, bathos and pathos. It is this combination of normally distinct properties that gives the verse its movement and edge. We feel illuminated, deepened, amused and perplexed, turn and turn about.

Furthermore, what is enacted in the poem, for Stevens, is the very nature of poetry itself. The poem is the enactment of poetry's essence, which is a thought with a strong romantic pedigree, as we will see presently. What this means is that *this* very poem

This endlessly elaborating poem
Displays the theory of poetry,
As the life of poetry.

In Stevens's verse, the frontier between poetry and poetics is constantly being criss-crossed *in* and *as* the work of the poem itself. As he writes in 'The Man with the Blue Guitar',

Poetry is the subject of the poem,
From this the poem issues and

To this returns. Between the two,
Between issue and return, there is

An absence in reality,
Things as they are. Or so we say.

(*PM* 143)

The nature of poetry is elicited through the poetic act itself, through 'the naked poem, the imagination manifesting itself in its domination of words' (*NA* viii). The theory of poetry – poetics – which a more harassing Coleridgean master would view as the theory of life, is performed in the specific poem insofar as that poem concerns itself with some real particular, with some object, thing or fact.

. . . Or so we say. A final qualification necessitated both by the evasiveness of what is being elicited by Stevens and its banality: things as they are only are in the act that says they are.

To forestall a possible misunderstanding, by philosophy I do not mean religious brooding. Although there are important religious concerns in Stevens, as when he says in a late poem that 'God and imagination are one' (*PM* 368), he is not a religious poet in the same way as, say, the later T.S. Eliot. Stevens fondly describes Eliot as 'an upright ascetic in an exceedingly floppy world'. Stevens is a somewhat floppier, gaudier, worldlier poet writing in the wake and complex cross-currents of romanticism.

What is romanticism? can arguably be reduced to the belief that art is the supreme medium for attaining the fundamental ground of life and that the problems of the modern world can be addressed and even reconciled in the production of a critically self-conscious artwork. This is what Friedrich Schlegel saw as the great novel of the modern world, a secular bible. Poetry written in the wake of romanticism – and I think that all poetry has to be written in romanticism's failure, but that's another story – is animated by the belief that poetry should take on to itself the existential burden of religious belief without the guarantee of religious belief. As Stevens expresses it at the beginning of his longest and most ambitious poem, 'Notes Toward a Supreme Fiction', 'The death of one god is the death of all' (*PM* 207).

Poetry has to be vitalized by the question of the ultimate meaning and value of life without claiming to know the metaphysical or theological answer to that question. Stevens makes this crystal clear in one of his *Adagia*, which were notebooks he kept in the 1930s and 1940s,

> After one has abandoned a belief in god, poetry is that
> essence which takes its place as life's redemption.
>
> *(OP* 185)

Poetry takes the place of religion as that medium which offers the possibility, or at least pursues the question, of life's redemption. It does this by producing fictions that return us to the sense of the world. It goes without saying that there is no sense in claiming, for Stevens, that there is anything that transcends the world. Although, in the final days of his illness from cancer, he was converted to Catholicism, I see this as the act of a dying, lonely man who confessed to 'a certain emptiness in his life' and who hadn't been on speaking terms with his wife for years.[2] In 'The Man with the Blue Guitar', he writes,

> Poetry
> Exceeding music must take the place
> Of empty heaven and its hymns,
>
> Ourselves in poetry must take their place,
> Even in the chattering of your guitar.
>
> *(PM* 135)

Poetry written in romanticism's wake is an anxious atheism, a restlessness with a religious memory and within a religious archive.

Stevens was self-consciously philosophical in his interests and much of his reading. He read widely in philosophy and his criticism abounds with references to classical texts, like Plato, and authors closer to his own time, like Bergson, William James and Russell. Some speculate on Whitehead's process philosophy as a possible influence. More certain is the influence of his teacher at Harvard, Santayana, to whom Stevens dedicated a moving and highly successful late poem, 'To an Old Philosopher in Rome' (*PM* 371–3). Stevens was also close to Jean Wahl, a hugely influential and unjustly neglected French philosopher active in the middle decades of the last century. Stevens was evidently a highly cultivated man. So what, you might exclaim, he was also a lawyer.[3]

Much more significantly, his entire work might be viewed as an extended elaboration of the guiding question of epistemology: the relation between thought and things, or mind and world. Let me explain. In the history of philosophy, this question has been posed in different ways in successive epochs. For the Pre-Socratic Parmenides, it is the question of the sameness between thought and Being, or between thinking and that which is. For Plato, it is the correspondence between the intellect and the forms, where knowledge of a thing is knowledge of the form of that thing. For Aquinas, it is the *adaequatio* between the intellect and things, where both persons and things are creatures created by a God himself uncreated. For Descartes and modern philosophy, it becomes the basic question of the theory of knowledge: namely, what is the relation between a thinking self or subject and the objects that appear to the subject.

The basic advance of Kant's epistemology at the end of the eighteenth century is that it does not suppose, as is supposed by both Plato and Descartes in quite different ways, that in order for knowledge to be possible there must be a correspondence between thoughts or mental representations and things in themselves, whether the realm of forms, the metaphysical realities of the soul, God and material substance, or simply a belief in the radical independence of reality from the mind, what Wilfrid Sellars calls 'the Myth of the Given'. After Kant, that which is true is that which is *taken* to be true, i.e. that which appears to a subject or self. Now, that which so appears might indeed refer to a thing in itself, but we can never be in a position to *know* this fact independently of how that fact *appears* to us. On Kant's picture, the realm of sensibility is our access to a world that is indeed real for us, but that world is always already shot through with conceptual content, it is articulated as such through the categories of the understanding and is dependent upon the spontaneity of the subject. This is why, as Kant says, 'the transcendental idealist is, therefore, an empirical realist'.[4]

It is in this Kantian lineage that Stevens has to be placed. Stevens can be said to be offering a poetic transposition and poetic undermining of the thesis of transcendental idealism, where the relation between thought and things or mind and world is redescribed as the relation between *imagination* and *reality*, the two master concepts of Stevens's poetics. Let me attempt a provisional definition of these terms. What is imagination? Imagination is that activity or, better, *power* in the sense of the German *Einbildungskraft*, of forming concepts beyond those derived from external objects. Understood in this way, the imagination is a power over external objects, or the transformation of the external into the internal through the work of subjective creation, a creation that is given sensuous form and is therefore rendered external in the work of art, the poem. I take it that this is what Hegel means when he speaks of art being born of the spirit and then reborn in being aesthetically regarded.[5] Art is born twice.

In one of his Athenaeum fragments, Friedrich Schlegel writes, 'No poetry, no reality'.[6] We should keep this in mind when reading Stevens, particularly as he places himself within a romantic tradition with its vast premise that the world might be transformed in and through a great artwork. So, no poetry, no reality: that is, our experience of the real is dependent upon the work of the poetic imagination. Yet, if there is no reality without poetry, then the inversion of Schlegel's remark would also seem to be true for Stevens, i.e. 'No reality, no poetry'. For Stevens, the poet must not lead us away from the real, where the solitary work of the imagination would result in fantasy or *fancy*. In Stevens's terminology, Coleridge's famous distinction between imagination and fancy might be redrawn in the following way: the poetic imagination must adhere to reality, whereas fancy works without reference to reality. As Stevens puts it, 'The real is only the base. But it is the base' (*OP* 187). So, the real is the base, it is the basis from which poetry begins, what Stevens calls the *materia poetica*, the matter of poetry, but it is only the base. One might say that reality is the necessary but not the sufficient condition for poetry, but it is absolutely necessary.

Dejected transcendental idealism

I am not saying that Stevens is simply a Kantian, but rather that he begins from Kantian premises read through romantic spectacles. That is, he begins from a perceived failure of Kantianism, from what might be called a *dejected transcendental idealism*. The shape of the thought I am after here can be found in Coleridge's 1802 'Dejection: An Ode', whose melancholy mood laments the abyssal distance between nature and the self, or between things-in-themselves and things-as-they-are-for-us. Coleridge famously writes,

> Though I should gaze for ever
> On that green light that lingers in the west:
> I may not hope from outward forms to win
> The passion and the life; whose fountains are within.

Therefore, the only meaning that we find in nature is that which we give to it,

> O Lady! we receive but what we give
> And in our life alone does Nature live.[7]

Nature in itself is that which resists the 'shaping spirit of imagination'. It is not for us and is simply indifferent to our existence. Thus, if transcendental idealism is true, it is only so *faute de mieux* and inspires dejection in us. The myth of the given might, after all, be a nice myth to believe in. I pursue the theme of dejection in detail in relation to the experience of nature in Stevens's very last poems, discussed in chapter 5. In these poems, Stevens's concern is not so much with the activity of poetic imagination, not with ideas about the thing, but with – in another obviously Kantian motif – the *thing itself*, with that bare, remote inhuman thing that lies beyond all human meaning-making.

Realism, anti-realism and phenomenology

The emphasis on reality in Stevens's poetry has an important philosophical consequence that has been nicely discussed in an essay by Sebastian Gardner.[8] Stevens's philosophical position, if one may call it that, cannot be assimilated to anti-realism, i.e. the belief that there is not (or there is no reference to) a subject-independent reality prior to language or discourse, which is an extremely fashionable and hegemonic view in the humanities and social sciences because of the influence of Saussure's linguistics and the so-called linguistic turn in Heidegger and the later Wittgenstein. Stevens has been widely interpreted as an anti-realist, for example in the influential interpretations of Harold Bloom and Joseph Riddel. The latter rightly reads Stevens's poetry as an 'act of the mind', but mental activity is wrongly understood in entirely solipsistic terms without reference to reality.[10] However, Riddel's claim for Stevens's anti-realism is evidenced more forthrightly in the sub-Nietzschean exuberance of a later essay, where reality is reduced to being the effect of language and the latter is understood as the early Nietzsche's mobile army of tropes, figures, metaphors and metonymies.[11] For Riddel, Stevens's poetry exhibits the 'tropological' quality of the real that reduces 'things as they are' to 'a chain of fictions'.[12] Bloom's anti-realism, which owes much to Schopenhauer, can be seen in microcosm in his interpretation of Stevens's important 1936 poem, 'The Idea of Order at Key West'. Bloom understands the concept of order in entirely solipsistic terms as the Schopenhauerian reduction of the world to an idea and the latter to consciousness. Poetry is here reduced to the effusions of a will that projects an illusory world of its own confection. For Bloom, like Riddel, the poem is entirely an act of the mind without reference to reality, a view that he ingeniously, but somewhat obsessively, traces back to Emerson, Whitman and the tradition of American transcendentalism.[13]

If Stevens were a straightforward anti-realist or linguistic idealist, then the only category in his poetics would be the imagination. But it is not, and his work begins from what Gardner terms a certain, oppressive or *contracted* sense of the real – what Hilary Putnam would call 'realism without a human face' – and attempts to put in its place a *transfigured* sense of the real, the real mediated through the creative power of imagination – 'realism with a human face'.[14] Stevens is not an anti-realist. The attempt to interpret him in this way reduces the work of the imagination to the frictionless spinning of fancy.

However, to say that Stevens is not an anti-realist does not entail that he is what we might call a transcendental realist. For the latter, all human activity is epiphenomenal to a subject-independent material realm explicable by the natural sciences. Such would be the contracted world, free from the cognitive, aesthetic and moral values that give colour and texture to the world we inhabit. Stevens's poetry is overwhelmingly concerned with reality but he believes that the real can be apprehended under different aspects or categories — the contracted, the transfigured. Simply stated, his conviction is that a poeticized, imaginatively transformed reality is both preferable to an inhuman, contracted and oppressive sense of reality and gives a truer picture of the relation humans entertain with the world.

Rightly, I think, Gardner seeks to link Stevens's transfigured sense of the real with Kant's thesis on transcendental idealism, that is, a world that is real for us, and hence consistent with empirical realism, but which has been produced in accordance with the categories of the understanding. The source of the categories lies in what Kant calls the transcendental or productive imagination, where 'Synthesis in general . . . is the mere result of the power of imagination'.[15] However, I believe that it might also be helpful to make a connection here with Heidegger's critique of the entire realism/anti-realism debate in *Being and Time*.[16] Heidegger criticizes both realism and anti-realism for having an inadequate account of the real, where the question of the 'reality' of the external world gets raised without any previous clarification of the phenomenon of world as that meaningful existential context that is most familiar and closest to us. As Stevens writes, 'Realism is a corruption of reality'.[17]

Stevens's poetic deepening of the thought of transcendental idealism might be said to lead him towards a more *phenomenological* sense of the real.[18] But what does this mean? What is phenomenology? Phenomenology is a description of things as they are that seeks to elicit the sense or significance of our practical involvement with the world. Again, more paradoxically stated, phenomenology brings

poetry, philosophy and life as it is

out the meaning of the fact that, in Merleau-Ponty's words, 'we are condemned to meaning'.[19] Phenomenology gives us the meaning of meaning. Or so we say. Phenomenological descriptions, if felici- ~~to whom?~~ tous, foreground things as they are experienced in the everyday world we inhabit, the real world in which we move and have our being, the world which fascinates and benumbs us. From this phenomenological perspective, the problem with Kant's approach is that it presupposes two things: first, a conception of the subject as what Kant calls the 'I think' that has, at the very least, a family resemblance to Descartes' *res cogitans*, even if it is a *cogito* without an *ergo sum*, where it performs a logical rather than an ontological function, i.e. what Kant calls 'the transcendental unity of apperception' is logically entailed from the fact that experience has a unity and coherence, but it does not imply any ontological insight into the nature of the self or soul. Second, it presupposes that the subject's relation to the objective world is mediated through representations, what Hegel calls 'picture thinking', Kant's and Fichte's *Vorstellungen*. If we place in question these two presuppositions, then it might lead us to abandon the entire epistemological construal of the relation of thought to things and mind to world. The world does not first and foremost show itself as an 'object' contemplatively and disinterestedly represented by a 'subject'. Rather, the world shows itself as a place in which we are completely immersed and from which we do not radically distinguish ourselves: 'Real and unreal are two in one'. What we might crudely call Stevens's philosophical position has been well stated by Charles Taylor in an essay entitled 'Overcoming Epistemology',

What you get underlying our representations of the world – the kind of things we formulate, for instance, in declarative sentences – is not further representations but rather a certain grasp of the world that we have as agents in it. This shows the whole epistemological construal of knowledge to be mistaken.[20]

Stevens's working assumption, which he owes once again to romanticism, is that the 'two-in-oneness' of the world is phenomenologically disclosed or reflectively transfigured as a world *not* in philosophy but through a poetic act, that is to say, in an artwork. It is the task of poetry to give us a sense of the world as it is, in the intricate evasions of as, directly and indirectly getting at the real in the edgings and inchings of final form. As Heidegger notes, alluding to the great poet Hölderlin, 'poetically, man dwells'.

Can poetry be philosophized?

So, in my view Stevens is philosophically significant because his verse recasts the basic problem of epistemology in a way that perhaps allows this problem to be cast away. What we might call his 'poetic epistemology' can be said to place in question the assumptions behind the traditional epistemological construal of the world.[21]

Yet, what intrigues me is that when Stevens tried, as he was invited to do in public lectures from the early 1940s onwards, to address the problem of the relation of poetry to philosophy in prose, the results were uneven, at best rather associative, and indeed poor in comparison to the power of his verse. Stevens's criticism is, in my view, at its strongest when it attains the condition of his poetry, as it does in an essay we shall examine presently, and at its weakest when it tries to approximate to more conventional academic discourse, as for example in the frankly disappointing 1951 University of Chicago lecture, 'A Collect of Philosophy', which was rejected – and rightly – by a prestigious philosophical journal which shall remain nameless. One is perhaps habituated to the idea that it is tricky, difficult, or simply downright futile to talk about poetry in philosophical terms, even poetry as self-consciously philosophical as that of Stevens. Philosophers appear rather flat-footed in comparison with the mercurial flight of the poets. But the oddity of Stevens's case is that he was himself somewhat inept at transliterating the philosophical content of his poetry into philo-sophical prose. A question I would like to keep in mind as we proceed is: why is this? What is it about the particular meditative poetic form that he developed that is able to carry genuine philo-sophical weight and yet which is impossible to translate into prose?

More troublingly, though, is it good for poetry to address philo-sophical problems so explicitly, even when it might be said to recast them or even cast them away? In my view it is, at least in the case of Stevens, but let me insert a cautionary note here with an anecdote. Some years ago, I took part in a workshop on Stevens where the other speaker was Frank Kermode. As many will know, Kermode was largely responsible for the initial reception of Stevens in the UK and the first book that I, like many others, read about Stevens was Kermode's introductory presentation.[22] After listening patiently to my rather philosophical take on Stevens's poetry, Kermode discreetly admonished me by admonishing Stevens's late verse for being too explicitly philosophical. In Kermode's view, the early poems from *Harmonium* are more successful as poetry than the later verse because they don't wear their metaphysics on their sleeve, as it were. Kermode reminded me that Stevens's first idea for a title for the *Collected Poems* of 1954 was *The Whole of Harmonium*. Now, I think Kermode is wrong in his judgement of the quality of the later poems, in particular the long poems and the late lyrics, though I take his point that perhaps it is better for poetry not to wear its philosophy so close to the surface, and to try to submerge those preoccupations into the particular grain of the poems. In relation to all of this, perhaps the following pages are only going to make matters worse. We shall see.

3

Sudden rightnesses

Let me try to set the stage for Stevens's poetry – and the stage is more than a mere metaphor, as we shall see – and for the entire problematic of modern poetry, by reading and discussing the poem of that name from the 1942 collection, *Parts of a World*: 'Of Modern Poetry',

> The poem of the mind in the act of finding
> What will suffice. It has not always had
> To find: the scene was set; it repeated what
> Was in the script.
>   Then the theatre was changed
> To something else. Its past was a souvenir.
>
> It has to be living, to learn the speech of the place.
> It has to face the men of the time and to meet

The women of the time. It has to think about war
And it has to find what will suffice. It has
To construct a new stage. It has to be on that stage
And, like an insatiable actor slowly and
With meditation, speak words that in the ear,
In the delicatest ear of the mind, repeat,
Exactly, that which it wants to hear, at the sound
Of which, an invisible audience listens,
Not to the play, but to itself, expressed
In an emotion as of two people, as of two
Emotions becoming one. The actor is
A metaphysician in the dark, twanging
An instrument, twanging a wiry string that gives
Sounds passing through sudden rightnesses, wholly
Containing the mind, below which it cannot descend,
Beyond which it has no will to rise.

                                  It must
Be the finding of a satisfaction, and may
Be of a man skating, a woman dancing, a woman
Combing. The poem of the act of the mind.

                                          (*PM* 174–5)

The problematic of modern poetry is succinctly stated in the poem's opening line which is then slightly modified as a refrain in the final line, 'The poem of the mind in the act of finding what will suffice'. This is as concise a definition of romanticism as one is likely to find. That is, modern poetry is an act of the mind, a conscious act of creation or genius that has to find what will suffice.

sudden rightnesses

Which is to say that what might suffice is not *given*, it is not a fact lying around for us to discover. This is why we are metaphysicians in the dark. The only light with which we might view objects has to be kindled by us, by our activity. So, the darkness here is not at all frightening, it is rather that if we are in the dark, then it is a question for us of *finding* what will suffice, what Stevens calls 'the finding of a satisfaction'.

Stevens gives a series of rather specific suggestions, if not quite a recipe, for what might suffice. The poem of the act of the mind has to be living, it has to speak the language of this place and be attuned to our climate. It has to face the men and women of the time and, which is something repeated at the end of the poem, it has to face them in their specific everyday activities, such as skating, dancing and combing. The modern poem *has* to do this because these men and women, at this time, performing these actions, are the poem's audience. Considerations of audience are vitally important here because what will suffice is not simply the imaginings of the poet. Rather, those imaginings, in order not to be mere fancy, have to correspond to the audience's sense of reality, a shared sense, a *sensus communis*. If the actor is a metaphysician in the dark, then he is only such for a living audience, otherwise the theatre would be truly dark.

Stevens goes on in line three, 'It has not always had to find: the scene was set; it repeated what was in the script'. That is, for the pre-modern poet, whatever 'modern' means here, the scene *was* set, the script *was* written, the facts *were* given. As such, the pre-modern poet could simply read from the script, and tell the stories of gods and heroes. He could compare the soul to a wingèd chariot, or, in

35

metaphysical terms, aspire to the Platonism of *scientia divina*, godlike knowledge. Then 'the theatre was changed to something else. Its past was a souvenir.' Stevens does not say when the scene was changed, but it is clear that the passage from ancient to modern poetry occurs when the theatre becomes a ruin, a ruin in which we moderns sit. As Friedrich Schlegel remarks, 'Many of the works of the ancients have become fragments. Many modern works are fragments as soon as they are written.'[1] Stevens continues the dramatic metaphor in the slightly later poem, 'Repetitions of a Young Captain',

A tempest cracked on the theatre. Quickly,
The wind beat in the roof and half the walls.
The ruin stood still in an external world. (. . .)
The people sat in the theatre, in the ruin,
As if nothing had happened.

(*CP* 306)

Metaphysics in the dark

One clumsy but compelling philosophical way of interpreting Stevens's thought here is in terms of the move from what is called *metaphysica specialis*, special metaphysics concerned with God, freedom and immortality, to *metaphysica generalis*, or the general metaphysics of Kant's transcendental idealism, discussed above. That is, if Kant decisively shows that the issues of the nature of God and soul are simply beyond our ken and are thus cognitively meaningless, then that does not exclude the possibility of a philosophy that would investigate into the conditions of possibility for what we actually do know. Such is the transcendental turn in philosophy. So conceived, the question of the relation of thought to things or mind to world can no longer be conceived in terms of some myth of the given, whether material or immaterial substance, but rather has to be conceived as radically subject-dependent, i.e. that which is, *is* only for the subject to whom it appears, even if what appears is real for us. As Hillis Miller puts it in a seminal early essay on Stevens, 'God is dead, therefore I am'.[2]

For Stevens, as for Kant, *reality is really real for a real audience of real people*, but it is wholly shot through with conceptual content whose ultimate source is the imagination. If Kant is right, then in Stevens's words, the metaphysical actor 'has to construct a new stage'. The stage upon which it appears is not one which was set for it, but one which it had to construct from the ruins, and Stevens insists, 'It has to be on that stage'. In the title of another of Stevens's poems, the thought would seem to be that 'The World is what you make of it' (*PM* 375). Yet, this world is not a thing of fancy, a figment or mere bubble. After building his own stage, the actor has to speak words that repeat exactly what he wants to hear, but which are listened to by an invisible audience, an audience, moreover, that does not listen to a play, but to itself, where audience and actor fuse together in an emotion. Modern poetry – and this is a theme to be explored in the next chapter – achieves truth through emotional identification, where actor and audience fuse, becoming two-in-one.

So what does a metaphysician in the dark do there in the dark? Does he grope for a light switch? No, he twangs. Stevens describes the metaphysical actor as,

(. . .) twanging a wiry string that gives
Sounds passing through sudden rightnesses, wholly
Containing the mind, below which it cannot descend,
Beyond which it has no will to rise.

Those familiar with Stevens's poetic symbolism will recognize that
the metaphysician in the dark is a member of the same family as
'The Man with the Blue Guitar', from the eponymous collection
published in 1936. The figure of the man bent over his guitar was
inspired by Picasso's 1903 'The Old Guitarist', which in turn
inspired David Hockney to produce an exquisite edition of the
poem illustrated with a series of etchings.[3] This 'shearsman' with his
blue guitar is also involved in a close dialogue with an audience, a
'they-self' which is also, as we have seen, 'it-self'.

They said, 'You have a blue guitar,
You do not play things as they are.'

The man replied, 'Things as they are
Are changed upon the blue guitar.'

And they said then, 'But play, you must,
A tune beyond us, yet ourselves,

A tune upon the blue guitar
Of things exactly as they are.'

Such is the whole enigma of modern poetry: how can something be both 'beyond us, yet ourselves'? The poet has to say things as they are, exactly as they are, as they are recognized by the men and women of the time. And yet, those things are changed and turned around upon the blue guitar, becoming beyond us, yet ourselves. When the man with the blue guitar twangs his wiry string harmoniously, when he finds the right note, then he will sound 'sudden rightnesses' and will achieve 'the finding of a satisfaction'. But what does this mean? What might rightness mean here? Four things come to mind:

1. The dark metaphysical activity of the poet is described in musical terms, where rightness would be a kind of harmony between mind and world. In this sense, our being-in-the-world would be experienced as emotional attunement, which is one rendering of Heidegger's notion of *Stimmung*, which is otherwise rather flatly rendered as 'mood'. Metaphysics in the dark is a kind of music, where rightness means sounding right.

2. Stevens seems to be proposing that dark metaphysical talk is only successful insofar as the sounds passing achieve *sudden* rightnesses, which is an arresting expression. Again the connection with music suggests itself, for a rightness is the experience of hitting the right note, finding what suffices, what strikes a chord, what satisfies, where one pauses while a sound passes into silence. In short, such rightness possesses the transience of music. It is something of a truism of Stevensiana – that is nonetheless true – to say that his poetry has the quality of music.[4] At times, in wonderfully sonorous

poems like 'To the One of Fictive Music' (*PM* 82–3), Stevens's words are like musical notes.

3. Lurking behind this notion of sudden rightness is a deeper observation, I think: namely, that if one accepts that metaphysics as *scientia divina* is impossible, then it seems to me that metaphysical talk can only live on in the dark, in the form of certain remarks which light up and render suddenly perspicuous certain perplexities we might have. In this sense, the dark metaphysical talk of the poet can momentarily focus the bewilderment to which most of us are wedded, and which passes for our inner life. As Henry James remarks, 'It seems probable that if we were never bewildered there would never be a story to tell about us.'[5] In such circumstances, rightness can only mean the felicity of hitting the right note, of saying something or telling a story that momentarily both harmonizes with our experience and submits that experience to what Wittgenstein would call 'aspect change' – a tune beyond us, yet ourselves.

4. Perhaps this is what Adorno is getting at when he speaks of metaphysical experience in reference to Proust's fascination with certain words: *Illiers, Trouville, Cabourg, Venice*, words which in a passing rightness produce an experience of *déjà vu* or *temps perdu* – something that happens to me when I hear the words 'Letchworth Garden City', 'Fingringhoe' or 'Biggleswade'.[6] Dark metaphysical talk becomes, in a deep sense, the sound of words. We will come back to this thought.

At its best, modern poetry achieves the experience of a sudden rightness that can be crystallized in a word, a name or a sound, the twanging of a blue guitar. At its worst, it does not. Such sound suffices by momentarily lighting up the everyday world,

> That music is intensest which proclaims
> The near, the clear and vaunts the clearest bloom.

> (*PM* 83)

Poetry intensifies experience by suddenly suspending it, withdrawing one from it, and lighting up not some otherworldly obscurities, but what Emerson in 'The American Scholar' calls 'the near, the low, the common'.[7] This allusion is helpful, for if Stevens's poetry is sublime, then it is a decidedly *American* sublime. In the poem of that name, Stevens writes,

> But how does one feel?
> One grows used to the weather,
> The landscape and that;
> And the sublime comes down
> To the spirit itself,

> The Spirit and space,
> The empty spirit
> In vacant space.

What wine does one drink?
What bread does one eat?

(*PM* 114)

The question posed in this poem is how might one stand in America to behold the sublime, 'To confront', as Stevens puts it in a Disneyesque allusion, 'the mockers / The mickey mockers / And plated pairs?'. Questioning is very much the issue here, namely that the sacramental symbols of Christianity, bread and wine, which are also the symbols of the Hölderlinian romanticism of 'Brod und Wein', have become questions and become questionable to us: 'What wine does one drink? / What bread does one eat?'. What exactly would constitute the meaning of the sacred and the sacramental in America? As Stevens puts it in a very late poem,

A mythology reflects its region, here
In Connecticut, we never lived in a time
When mythology was possible.

(*PM* 398)

The appeal of Connecticut for Stevens is the slightness of its beauty and the hardness, thrift and frugality that this unforgiving landscape imposed on its colonists (*OP* 302–4). And perhaps here one finds a possible response to the question of the American sublime. As Stevens puts it, 'the sublime comes down / To the spirit itself', in a way that is at least analogous to the movement from ancient to modern poetry, or special to general metaphysics described above. The meaning of the American sublime might simply consist in the

sudden rightnesses

mind growing used to 'the weather, / The landscape and that'. It is this seemingly throwaway 'and that' which interests me, where the mind has to find a satisfaction, what suffices, right here, right now, in a poetic act that cannot take it away from the here and now.

Poetry, for Stevens, is the description of a particular – the wine, the bread, the 'and that' – in the radiant atmosphere produced by the imagination. Poetic acts are acts of the mind, which describe recognizable things, but which vary the appearance of those things, changing the aspect under which they are seen. Poetry transfigures a common, but contracted, reality. In a phrase – an idealistic thesis, indeed – that Stevens repeated, poetry '. . . is an illumination of a surface, the movement of a self in the rock' (*NA* viii/*OP* 257). As such, poetry is an elevation, an enlargement of life. But what is essential is that poetry should produce this elevation 'in words free from mysticism' (*NA* viii), in words that do not purport to any intuition of a transcendent reality, in words appropriate to our climate of the near, the low and the imperfect, in poor weather and without mythology. Late in *The Necessary Angel*, Stevens touches on the theme of *decreation*, borrowed from Simone Weil. The modern reality of the modern poet is a reality of decreation, 'in which our revelations are not the revelations of belief, but the precious portents of our powers' (*NA* 174).[8] In other words, God is dead, therefore I am. The problem is that it is not at all clear who I am.

4

Wallace Stevens's intimidating thesis

As you may have noticed, I passed over the mention of war in 'Of Modern Poetry'. The modern poem also has to think about finding what might suffice in a time of war. We might ponder the meaning of war in Stevens and this will be at the centre of my discussion of Malick. War is a theme that recurs in Stevens's work, particularly and unsurprisingly during the 1940s. In the poem that precedes 'Of Modern Poetry', 'Man and Bottle', he writes,

> It has to be content to reason concerning war,
> It has to persuade that war is part of itself,
> A manner of thinking, a mode
> Of destroying, as the mind destroys.

> (*PM* 174)

Parts of a World concluded with the long poem, 'Examination of the Hero in a Time of War', and for the original publication Stevens added a half-page prose statement on the poetry of war. He writes, 'The immense poetry of war and the poetry of a work of the imagination are two different things' (*PM* 206). For Stevens, in the violent reality of war, *consciousness* takes the place of the imagination. By consciousness, he would appear to mean that the poetry of war is obviously and directly concerned with observation and fact, with what he calls 'heroic fact', rather than the endless struggle with fact that characterizes the imagination. In a time of war, imagination appears impotent and we are overwhelmed with the desire for fact. Whilst I find this distinction less than wholly perspicuous, it does raise the important question of the environment, the context in the midst of which the poetic imagination finds itself. As Hölderlin wrote at the beginning of the nineteenth century, with a question that Heidegger made his own at the darkest moment of the twentieth century, *'Wozu Dichter in dürftiger Zeit?'*, 'What are poets for in a time of dearth?'.[1]

I would like to consider this question by turning to Stevens's sole volume of criticism, *The Necessary Angel*, which begins with a lecture given at Princeton in 1942, 'The Noble Rider and the Sound of Words'. Here, Heidegger's time of dearth becomes 'a leaden time . . . a world that does not move for the weight of its own heaviness' (*NA* 63). The lecture is dominated by the presence of war, the war that the USA had entered in the previous year, and this mood defines Stevens's central theme, which is what he calls 'the pressure of reality'. The latter is described in various ways, not just as the proximity of war, but as the continual pressure of the news, and the emerging sense of a shrunken world girdled by the media, where 'there is no distance' (*NA* 18). Stevens writes,

Wallace Stevens's intimidating thesis

All the great things have been denied and we live in an
intricacy of new and local mythologies, political, economic, poetic, which are asserted with an ever-enlarging
incoherence.

(*NA* 17)

Plus ça change, one might shrug. But perhaps it never changes, perhaps
our experience of the present is always dominated by this feeling of
pressure. Unless it should be forgotten, ours is a time of war.
Understood in this way, Stevens's description might apply as well to
our time as it does to his. He writes, rightly, 'It is one of the peculi-
arities of the imagination that it is always at the end of an era'
(*NA* 22). Perhaps we always feel ourselves to be at the end of Pope's
Dunciad, where 'Universal darkness buries all'.

Stevens's concern is how the imagination might resist the pressure of reality. This is organized around the theme of nobility.
Poetry is an ennobling of things through words, it is '. . . the
supreme use of language' (*NA* 19). Stevens adds, 'There is no element
more conspicuously absent from contemporary poetry than nobility' (*NA* 35). For him, and this is rather controversial, the possibility
of nobility goes together with the refusal of the attempt to reduce
the function of poetry to social and political concerns. Stevens is
blunt, 'In this area of my subject I might be expected to speak of the
social, that is to say sociological or political obligation of the poet.
He has none' (*NA* 27). Stevens persistently defended the idea of pure
poetry, as for example in the jacket statement to the 1936 collection
Ideas of Order, where in the depths of the great depression he sought
to separate the idea of poetic order from questions of economic,

47

social and political order (*OP* 222). To conflate these orders would be to confuse imagination with consciousness. It should not be forgotten that Stevens is the author of a poem entitled, 'The Revolutionists Stop for Orangeade' (*CP* 102).

This is not quite as reactionary as it sounds. For Stevens, the true subject matter of poetry is life and the role of the poet is 'to help people live their lives' (*NA* 30). What this means concretely for Stevens is that poetry should provide resistance to the pressure of reality through the activity of the imagination, 'The more realistic life may be, the more it needs the stimulus of the imagination' (*OP* 223). The nobility of poetry lies in its pressing back against the pressure of reality, a nobility that is nothing more, as we saw above, than the sound of words, such as Wordsworth's

> This City now doth, like a garment, wear
> The beauty of the morning, silent, bare . . .

(*NA* 31)

This noble pressing back is also a *violence*, as Stevens readily admits, 'A violence from within that protects us from a violence without' (*NA* 36). It is the violence of the imagination bringing about felt variations in the appearances of things through what we called above dark metaphysical talk. For Stevens, it is this violence which gives to life the supreme fictions 'without which we are unable to conceive of it' (*NA* 31). The task of poetry is the writing of a supreme fiction.

These insights are significantly deepened in a lecture from the following year, 'The Figure of the Youth as Virile Poet', which is Stevens's finest piece of criticism and which, in some passages, bears comparison with his verse. He begins in a rather minor key, with the contrast between philosophy, as what he calls 'the official view of being', and poetry, as 'the unofficial view of being'. He goes on, somewhat superficially – after all, Stevens was not above that – to identify philosophy with reason and poetry with the imagination, where a comparison between the two domains unsurprisingly results in the assertion of the superiority of the latter over the former. The contrast between philosophy and poetry is rather lightly handled and is largely based on borrowings from various quoted authorities, such as Russell, Bergson and William James. Stevens makes the rather flippant assertion that 'the philosopher proves that the philosopher exists. The poet merely enjoys existence' (*NA* 56). It is clear which existence is preferred by Stevens, and in the imaginative atmosphere of the poet the philosopher is an alien with his gaunt use of reason. This is a polite way of saying that Stevens sometimes betrayed a rather impoverished conception of philosophy and expressed this view in a rather associative way. This becomes particularly annoying in the 1951 lecture, 'A Collect of Philosophy', where we are treated to unadorned extracts from Stevens's correspondence with Paul Weiss, Jean Wahl and Jean Paulhan and half-digested lumps of Rogers's *A Student's History of Philosophy* and Alexander's *Space, Time and Deity* (*OP* 271–6). Thin gruel indeed!

Matters begin to get more interesting when Stevens broaches the question of poetic truth. Poetry is truthful when it is in agreement with the world; that is, an agreement between imagination and reality, a finding of what will suffice, a satisfaction. Such agreement is emotional for Stevens – it is a *felt* agreement. Poetic truth is an agreement with reality in what Stevens calls, and it is a favourite nickname, a *mundo*. The latter is the environment created by the poet, what Stevens often describes in this lecture and his poetry as the *radiant* atmosphere of the poet. What the poet does is to create a *mundo*, a specific habitat with an identifiable voice, personae, climate and set of objects. Such an imagining elevates and liberates both the poet and the reader who finds vitality in this world, who finds in it some affluence of the planet they inhabit.

There then follows an extraordinary passage, where Stevens asks us to enter into a thought-experiment, to enter the *mundo* of the poet, that radiant atmosphere. How do things look when we inhabit the world of the poet? At the end of a rather unhelpful brief discussion of metaphysics, Stevens asks an extremely long and tortuous question,

And having ceased to be metaphysicians, even though we have acquired something from them as from all men, and standing in the radiant and productive atmosphere, and examining first one detail of that world, one particular, and then another, as we find them by chance, and observing many things that seem to be poetry without any interven- tion on our part, as, for example, the blue sky, and noting, in any case, that the imagination never brings anything into the world but that, on the contrary, like the personality of the

Wallace Stevens's intimidating thesis

> poet in the act of creating, it is no more than a process, and
> desiring with all the power of our desire not to write falsely,
> do we not begin to think of the possibility that poetry is
> only reality, after all, and that poetic truth is a factual truth,
> seen, it may be, by those whose range in the perception of
> fact – that is, whose sensibility – is greater than our own?
>
> (*NA* 59)

It is unclear to me whether the last pronoun of this passage is intended to include or exclude Stevens. But what we see when we take on board the poet's *mundo* is that the things around us that make up the world seem to be poetry without any intervention on our part. For example, the blue sky: the blue sky is poetry, but it is also the blue sky, as it is. That is, the power of the poetic imagination produces a world that we recognize as our world, which is not a fantasy world or thing of fancy. If the poet's world is true, then this is because it attempts to be true to the perceived contours of the world we actually inhabit: this place, this blue sky, this clear water in a brilliant bowl, this green grass, this leafless tree, these sweet berries, my cat Jeoffrey. It is only by agreeing with reality that the imagination has vitality. As Stevens succinctly puts it in the *Adagia*, the task of poetry is 'To touch with the imagination in respect to reality' (*OP* 287).

Stevens then asks us: if we indeed accept that we stand within the radiant *mundo* of the poet (and everything hangs on that 'if'; you can't force someone to take on board a poetic vision, and there is no accounting for taste), then are we not obliged to accept 'the possibility that poetic truth is a factual truth'? Namely, that true poetry, the work of the imagination that touches reality, is a poetry of fact, of fact created in a fiction. If we take the small leap of faith implied in that 'if', then we are no longer inhabiting our ordinary world, but the *mundo* of the poet, namely someone, 'whose range in the perception of fact – that is, whose sensibility – is greater than our own'. The consequence of Stevens's argumentation is that the truth that we experience when the poet's fictive imaginings are in agreement with reality is a truth of fact. But it is an *enlarged* world of fact: things as they are, but beyond us.

The imagination of life – an intimidating thesis

Poetry is a queer business. The poet invites us to inhabit a world, a radiant atmosphere, a world shot through by the singular power of the poetic imagination. When we accept this invitation and begin to see things through the poet's *mundo*, then we might exclaim – and the following words are set apart in italics in the text of 'The Figure of the Youth as Virile Poet', as if spoken by another personage,

> *No longer do I believe that there is a mystic muse, sister of the Minotaur. This is another of the monsters I had for nurse, whom I have wasted. I am myself a part of what is real, and it is my own speech and the strength of it, this only, that I hear or ever shall.*

(*NA* 60)

The world is what you make of it and reality is the echo of imagination's power. Yet, as I have insisted, this fictive world is a world of fact, it is a world with which we are already familiar, otherwise the

Wallace Stevens's intimidating thesis

conjurings of the poet would be meaningless. It is a world of fact given to us by someone with a range of sensibility greater than our own, a poetic sensibility. So, stranger still, it is an *enlarged* world of fact, an exquisite environment of fact, what Stevens calls 'an incandescence of the intelligence'. The words of the poet widen the panorama of our world. We see more and see further through the poet's eyes.

The world that we inhabit is neither a bubble of subjective fancy à la Bloom, nor an epiphenomenon to an alien, subject-independent realm à la Quine. Epistemologically speaking, both anti-realism and transcendental realism are wrong. Against H.D. Lewis's 1946 paper, 'On Poetic Truth', Stevens argues that poetry has to do not with a bare, alien reality, but with a reality with which we are already in contact, a solid existing reality, a world shot through with our cognitive, moral and aesthetic values. He writes, 'no fact is bare fact, no individual fact is a universe in itself' (*NA* 96). This poeticized version of transcendental idealism is hypothesized in the following terms,

> It comes to this, that poetry is part of the structure of reality.
> If this has been demonstrated, it pretty much amounts to
> saying that the structure of poetry and the structure of
> reality are one or, in effect, that poetry and reality are one, or
> should be. This may be less thesis than hypothesis.
>
> (*NA* 81)

Despite this coy quasi-retraction and qualification, we are here being brought close to what Stevens calls his *intimidating thesis*. What

53

is this thesis? He writes, 'poetry is the imagination of life' (*NA* 65). This entails that there is no such thing as bare alien fact, what Stevens calls 'absolute fact'. Rather,

> . . . absolute fact includes everything that the imagination includes. This is our intimidating thesis.
>
> (*NA* 61)

Absolute fact is not absolute, in the sense of being absolved from any relation to the imagination; it is simply the *arrière-pays* of the imagination and therefore relative to its power. Stevens illustrates this in a disarmingly prosaic and charming manner,

> One sees demonstrations of this everywhere. For example, if we close our eyes and think of a place where it would be pleasant to spend a holiday, and if there slide across the black eyes, like a setting on a stage, a rock that sparkles, a blue sea that lashes, and hemlocks in which the sun can merely fumble, this inevitably demonstrates, since the rock and sea, the wood and sun are those that have been familiar to us in Maine, that much of the world of fact is the equivalent of the world of the imagination, because it looks like it.
>
> (*NA* 61)

Poetry is the imagination of life. That is, it is the imagination of life as it is, the coastline of Maine, Suffolk, Carthage or wherever. The imagined coastline is true to the factual coastline simply 'because it looks like it'. Yet, it is life elevated, a world of fact enlarged and rendered radiant through the sound of words. Poetry is life as it is, ourselves yet beyond us.

Words of the world are the life of the world and poetry is the highest use of those words. Without poetry we are diminished, we become mere 'castratos of moon-mash'. Poetry is like the light which illuminates objects in the world, it is the unseen condition for seeing, unseen until seen with the poet's eyes and then seen anew. Like light, it adds nothing but itself. Close to the heat of that light, we can be said to live more intensely.

5
The twofold task of poetry

We find an order in things. This is not an order that is given, but one that we give it. Poetry reorders the order that we find in things. It gives us back things exactly as they are, but beyond us, 'a tune beyond us, yet ourselves' (*PM* 133). The imaginative reordering of the world through the sound of words both touches a common reality and gives us that reality back under a new aspect, anew, transfigured. As Stevens writes in 'The Idea of Order at Key West' from 1936, perhaps his most Wordsworthian poem, poetry is a process of 'Arranging, deepening and enchanting' (*PM* 98). Poetry rearranges the arrangement of things that we find in the world, and deepens it, making it more intense and profound. Enchanting should be understood literally, as singing the world into existence. As the poet and his interlocutor, Ramon Fernandez, remarks in the same poem,

> Then we,
> As we beheld her, striding there alone,

Knew that there never was a world for her
Except the one she sang and, singing, made.

(PM 98)

Poetry is the enchantment of the world, the incantation of reality
under the spell of imagination, a world spelled out through words,
but still a world for us. In this sense, poetry is a sort of sorcery, a
transfiguration of the world in words which gives us what Stevens
would call 'the idea of order', even if this order is fictional. Not
that it is *only* fictional, for Stevens's profounder point is that all possible orderings of reality are fictional. With this is mind, we might,
if I may be so bold, formulate the twofold task of poetry:

Fact = act, poesis

1. Poetry permits us to see fiction as fiction, to see the fictiveness or
contingency of the world. It reveals the idea of order which we
imaginatively impose on reality. Plainly stated, the world is what
you make of it. The fact of the world is a *factum*: a deed, an act, an
artifice. Such is what we might call the *critical* task of poetry, which I
have tried to link to the Kantian critique of *metaphysica specialis*. This
is perhaps what Stevens has in mind when he writes in the *Adagia*,

> The final belief is to believe in a fiction, which you know to
> be a fiction, there being nothing else. The exquisite truth is
> to know that it is a fiction and that you believe it willingly.

(OP 189)

This is a thought that is picked up in 'Asides on the Oboe',

The prologues are over. It is a question, now,
Of final belief. So, say that final belief
Must be in a fiction. It is time to choose.

(*PM* 187)

On the one hand, poetry can bring us to this exquisite truth, namely that fiction is the truth of truth, a view that does not lead to anti-realism or linguistic idealism, as many of Stevens's interpreters conclude, and that does not exclude questions of truth, as I hope to have shown.

2. However, the second task of poetry is to give '. . . to life the supreme fictions without which we are unable to conceive of it'. Beyond the critical function described above, we might describe this as the *therapeutic* task of poetry. Namely, poetry is 'one of the enlargements of life' (*NA* viii). Poetry offers a possible form of redemption, a redemption that brings us back to the fictiveness of the world and which saves the sense of the world for us. At this point, we might consider what is arguably Stevens's most important, ambitious and difficult poem, 'Notes toward a Supreme Fiction'. Emphasis should be put here on the fact that these are only notes toward this fiction, and that Stevens does not offer the latter to us whole and ready made,

It is possible, possible, possible. It must
Be possible.

(*PM* 230)

Stevens's work, and it shares this characteristic with its great romantic precursors like Coleridge, is a poetry of notes, often musical notes.[1] Yet, the paradox is that Stevens does not offer us an anti-realist celebration of the fictionality of the fictional, but rather notes toward a *supreme* fiction. That is, a fiction that would be true and in which we might believe. In the *Adagia*, this is what Stevens calls,

> The exquisite environment of fact. The final poem will be
> the poem of fact in the language of fact.
>
> (*OP* 190)

But, he concludes with a singular dialectical twist of meaning, '. . . it will be a poem of fact not realized before' (*OP* 190). Thus, to write the supreme fiction, the supreme unreality, is paradoxically,

> To find the real,
> To be stripped of every fiction except one,
> The fiction of an absolute . . .
>
> (*PM* 230)

The supreme fiction is the fiction of a fact. It is in such a fiction that we can finally believe. It is the type of fiction that we can take to be true.

6

The thing itself and its seasons

'Someday someone must write an opus on the
effects of climate on the imagination.'[1]

The above is a sketch, with perhaps a little too much local colour,
of what we might call 'the official view' of Stevens's art. I wrote it in
the hope of getting Stevens right by taking him at his word and
thereby trying to oppose what I see as an easy, anti-realist *doxa*
in the interpretation of his work. Far from being an anti-realist,
Stevens is attempting to write a poetry of reality, where imagination
touches reality, transfiguring the reality that it touches. I have
emphasized the Kantian and romantic lineage of this thought.
Philosophically expressed, Stevens allows us to recast the basic
problem of epistemology in a way that lets that problem be cast
away. This much, I hope, is clear.

Yet, there is a profound paradox in Stevens's art, which I would
like to pursue in this chapter. As we have seen, Stevens's intimidating thesis is that poetry is the imagination of life and, one might
aphorize, *where there is no imagination, there no thing may be.* But in

Stevens's very last poems, the poems he grouped under the title *The Rock* in the *Collected Poems* in 1954 and in other lyrics from the same period, something rather different is going on. In these extraordinary poems, the overwhelming concern is not with the activity of the poetic imagination, not with ideas about the thing, but – in another obviously Kantian motif – with *the thing itself*, the bare remote inhuman thing that lies beyond all human understanding and meaning-making. This is what Stevens calls 'the rock', the thing itself unadorned by poetic incantation and gaudy decoration. Various related objects repeatedly appear onstage in these late lyrics: winter trees, a pond, the sun, fallen leaves, sundry birds. I shall try to show that what is at stake in this choice of natural objects is a return to what Stevens calls 'The Plain Sense of Things' (*PM* 382).

This is not to say that this concern with the thing itself is absent in Stevens's earlier verse. Far from it. The prospect of reality without the transfiguring power of the imagination is a recurring theme in Stevens's verse. To pick three examples from *Harmonium*, 'The Comedian as the Letter C' begins by imagining the world without imagination (*PM* 58) and 'The Snow Man' ends by beholding the 'Nothing that is not there and the nothing that is' (*PM* 54). In a peculiarly haunting short poem, 'Nuances of a Theme By Williams', Stevens adds ten elliptical lines of verse to four lines by his great and conflictual contemporary, William Carlos Williams, and tries to imagine the sun without imagination,

> Shine alone, shine nakedly, shine like bronze,
> that reflects neither my face nor any inner part

of my being, shine like fire,
that mirrors nothing.

(PM 39).

As J. Hillis Miller wisely points out, 'At times (Stevens) is unequivocally committed to bare reality. At other times he repudiates reality and sings the praises of imagination.'[2] Indeed, it is plausible to read Stevens's entire poetic production in terms of an oscillation between two poles and two aesthetic temptations: on the one hand, the imagination seizing hold of reality, and on the other, reality resisting the imagination. I will come back to this thought in my conclusion. Yet, that said, in Stevens's late lyrics there is a directness, a sparseness, a simple lack of gaudiness and an almost despairing beauty that is lacking in the earlier verse. One cannot imagine the late Stevens writing,

> Chieftain Iffucan of Azcan in caftan
> Of tan with henna hackles, halt!

(PM 75)

One after another, the late lyrics strive to evoke a reality that retreats from the advances of language. Some acute commentators, such as Roy Harvey Pearce and Randall Jarrell, have picked up on the atypical timbre of the late verse. Yet, no one appears to have picked up on the shift of philosophical weight to be found in these poems.[3]

The four seasons

Let's begin with the poem to which I have already alluded more than once, 'Not Ideas about the Thing but the Thing Itself', the poem which concludes the *Collected Poems*,

At the earliest ending of winter,
In March, a scrawny cry from outside
Seemed like a sound in his mind.

He knew that he heard it,
A bird's cry, at daylight or before,
In the early March wind.

The sun was rising at six,
No longer a battered panache above snow . . .
It would have been outside.

It was not from the vast ventriloquism
Of sleep's faded papier-mâché . . .
The sun was coming from outside.

That scrawny cry – It was
A Chorister whose c preceded the choir.
It was part of the colossal sun,

Surrounded by its choral rings,
Still far away. It was like
A new knowledge of reality.

(*PM* 388)

the thing itself and its seasons

The first thing to note is the time of the poem, its season. This is the chilly New England March, 'the earliest ending of winter'. As readers of Stevens will know, his work employs a symbolic calendar of the seasons. Many of the very late lyrics take place in late autumn, 'after the leaves have fallen', in snowy winter, or the very early spring. Allow me a word on this calendar. As can be seen in a poem like 'Credences of Summer', summer is the time when the mind lays by its trouble, with

> spring's infuriations over and a long way
> To the first autumnal inhalations . . .

> (*PM* 287)

We might define summer with Frank Kermode as '. . . the season of the physical paradise, the full human satisfaction', or with Sebastian Gardner as '. . . the world apprehended in the full blaze of what Stevens calls imagination'.[4] Such a full satisfaction would be the assimilation of reality into the imagination in a moment of complete transport and delight, the romantic reconciliation of art and life through the poetic imagination. As Stevens puts it, 'The world is larger in summer' (*PM* 376) because the imagination finds what suffices by showing its domination over reality.

By contrast, winter is the season of hard reality, of the world contracted into the absence of imagination, where the human subject is powerless before an oppressive, violent and indifferent reality. As Stevens puts it in the earlier 'Man and Bottle', in an echo of 'Of Modern Poetry',

The mind is the great poem of winter, the man,
Who, to find what will suffice,
Destroys romantic tenements
Of rose and ice . . .

(*PM* 173)

In winter, the imagination will not suffice and no satisfaction can be found. A beautiful late poem, 'A Discovery of Thought' begins,

At the Antipodes of Poetry, dark winter,
When the trees glitter with that which despoils them . . .

(*PM* 366)

Gardner interestingly evokes this world of winter as the contracted world of transcendental realism.[5] But what is missing from Gardner's otherwise compelling account is any consideration of the seasons of autumn and particularly early spring. Examples are legion: 'The Plain Sense of Things' begins 'After the leaves have fallen' in a 'blank cold' which signifies the 'end of the imagination' (*PM* 382). 'Lebensweisheitspielerei' begins,

Weaker and weaker, the sunlight falls
In the afternoon. The proud and the strong
Have departed.

(*PM* 383)

Yet, it is in this 'poverty of autumnal space' that we 'the unaccomplished' become 'The finally human natives of a dwindled sphere'

the thing itself and its seasons

(*PM* 383–4). 'Vacancy in the Park' begins 'March . . . someone has walked across the snow', and in 'Long and Sluggish Lines' Stevens writes, '. . . Wanderer, this is the pre-history of February'. What is taking place here is that, in the words of 'The Green Plant',

> The effete vocabulary of summer
> No longer says anything.

(*CP* 506)

(That is, we can no longer believe in the beautiful romantic dream of the power of the imagination.)

What is interesting about the seasons of late autumn and early spring is that they are a denial of both the worlds of winter and summer, both the contraction of hard reality and its full trans-figuration in imagination. These transitional seasons permit a more minimal, impoverished but perhaps credible transfiguration of the everyday, where the relation between imagination and reality takes place in the tension between contraction and transfiguration. It is, I believe, in terms of such a minimal transfiguration that Stevens envisages a return to the plain sense of things. In the words of the latter poem, although in the blank cold of March it is 'as if / We had come to an end of the imagination', Stevens crucially goes on to add that 'the absence of the imagination had / Itself to be imagined'. As Beckett put it in an important short prose piece, 'Imagination Dead Imagine'; which should be read as both a state-ment of a condition (the imagination is dead) and an imperative (imagine!). In these transitional seasons, we have to accustom our-selves to more minimal transfigurations that turn us to things in their ordinariness, sparseness and hardiness, the very Americanness of the sublime.

We find an echo of this ordinariness in the seemingly slight late lyric, 'Song of Fixed Accord',

Rou-cou spoke the dove,
Like the sooth lord of sorrow,
Of sooth love and sorrow,
And a hail-bow, hail-bow,
To this morrow.

She lay upon the roof,
A little wet of wing and woe,
And she rou-ed there,
Softly she piped among the suns
And their ordinary glare,

The sun of five, the sun of six,
Their ordinariness,
And the ordinariness of seven,
Which she accepted
Like a fixed heaven,

Not subject to change . . .
Day's invisible beginner,
The lord of love and of sooth sorrow,
Lay on the roof
And made much within her.

(*PM* 519–20)

the thing itself and its seasons

In the almost comic sing-song form of the poem, the melancholy cooing of the dove announces the dim glow of the sun. The insomniac eyes of the poet regard the sun of five, of six, of seven o'clock in its ordinariness, which echoes with the rising of the sun at six in 'Not Ideas about the Thing'. Returning to the latter poem, at the March day's beginning, the sun rises and there is a cry, '. . . a scrawny cry from outside / Seemed like a sound in his mind'. But the key word here is 'seemed'. The cry is not the imagination's echo in reality, 'It was not from the vast ventriloquism / Of sleep's faded papier-mâché . . . '. It is a bird's cry coming from outside. This is the thing itself, not ideas about it.

The cry of things that do not transcend themselves

I would like to stay a while with this thought of the cry. 'The Song of Fixed Accord' finds a direct echo in another late lyric, 'The Dove in Spring', with the reappearance of our sleepless dove and insomniac poet. It might be stretching the reader's tolerance just a little to hear in the 'brooder, brooder' of the opening line not just the cooing of the dove, but also the suggestion that the dove is the *Bruder* of the poet,

> Brooder, brooder, deep beneath its walls –
> A small howling of the dove
> Makes something of the little there,

The little and the dark, and that
In which it is and that in which
It is established. There the dove

Makes this small howling, like a thought
That howls in the mind or like a man
Who keeps seeking out his identity

In that which is and is established . . . It howls
Of the great sizes of an outer bush
And the great misery of the doubt of it,

Of stripes of silver that are strips
Like slits across a space, a place
And state of being large and light.

There is this bubbling before the sun
This howling at one's ear, too far
For daylight and too near for sleep.

(PM 385)

Here the 'Rou-cou' of the dove has become 'a small howling', a word repeated five times in the poem. This is a very odd choice of word, and suggests something more ominous and alien than cooing. And then, with exactly the same run of thought as in 'Not Ideas about the Thing', this small howling is 'like a thought / That howls in the mind'. But it is not in the mind, it is the howling of the dove *an sich,* as it were. Although this is a howling that is 'at one's ear', it is

the thing itself and its seasons

'too far for daylight and too near for sleep'. The cry is coming from outside, it is the chorister's 'c' that precedes the choir of the colossal sun. It is the howling of the thing itself.

In what is arguably the best of Stevens's late lyrics, 'The Course of a Particular', the cry is that of leaves and the time is once again the beginning of 'the nothingness of winter',

> Today the leaves cry, hanging on branches swept by wind,
> Yet the nothingness of winter becomes a little less.
> It is still full of icy shades and shapen snow.
>
> The leaves cry . . . One holds off and merely hears the cry.
> It is a busy cry, concerning someone else.
> And though one says that one is part of everything,
>
> There is a conflict, there is a resistance involved;
> And being part is an exertion that declines:
> One feels the life of that which gives life as it is.
>
> The leaves cry. It is not a cry of divine attention,
> Nor the smoke-drift of puffed-out heroes, nor human cry.
> It is the cry of leaves that do not transcend themselves,
>
> In the absence of fantasia, without meaning more
> Than they are in the final finding of the ear, in the thing
> Itself, until, at last, the cry concerns no one at all.

(*PM* 367)

The leaves cry, and the poet stands and hears their busy cry. The temptation of the imagination – if poetry is the imagination of life – is to say that 'one is part of everything' and therefore that this cry is a sound in the mind, an idea. But, as with the other poems we have looked at, the cry of the leaves is not a human cry, nor is it a symbol of God, the gods or puffed-out heroes. It is simply the cry of leaves that appear to reach out to us, but which do not transcend themselves. It is the cry of matter mattering regardless of whether it matters to us. The leaves *are*, but they are not for *us*. All that they mean, like the howling of the dove, is that which is found in the ear that hears, in the absence of fantasia, without the conjurings of the imagination. The poet hears the thing itself without the meaning-making work of the imagination.

In the central lines of the poem, what is being acknowledged is the resistance of things, of leaves, of birds, of the colossal sun. Stevens would seem to be accepting that one is simply *not* part of everything and that the feeling of being part of the whole – let's call it the Pantheist temptation – is 'an exertion that declines', a force of desire that lessens. I will come back to this theme presently, but it is difficult not to recall that these are amongst the last poems of a man in his mid-seventies. There is a palpable sense of withdrawal and res-ignation in these late lyrics. He writes, 'One feels the life of that which gives life as it is'. Life is given as it is, and it has to be received as such, until the moment it is taken away. The violence of the imagination's counter-movement against the pressure of reality that defined Stevens's art seems to have become pacific and calm. Reality presses in without oppressing the self. In their utter simplicity, these poems try to say things as they are given, things themselves as they are heard in the ear without meaning anything. To return to 'Not Ideas about the Thing', the cry of things is *like* a new knowledge of reality, but it is *not* in any sense a knowledge understood as the unity of concept and intuition. What we witness in these late lyrics is intuitions overflowing concepts without the source of the intuition, the thing itself, being in any sense assimilable by the mind.

The mere thereness of things

My guess – and it is no more than that – is that what Stevens is about in these late poems is what we might call *the poetry of the antipodes of poetry*. It is a sort of anti-poetry. That is, it is the poetry of that which Stevens's intimidating thesis seems to place out of bounds, the realm of absolute fact, that which decisively escapes the appropriative powers of the imagination. In Stevens's very last poem, this realm receives a heavily metaphysical name, 'Of Mere Being',

> The palm at the end of the mind,
> Beyond the last thought, rises
> In the bronze decor,
>
> A gold-feathered bird
> Sings in the palm, without human meaning,
> Without human feeling, a foreign song.
>
> You know then that it is not the reason
> That makes us happy or unhappy.
> The bird sings. Its feathers shine.

The palm stands on the edge of space.
The wind moves slowly in the branches.
The bird's fire-fangled feathers dangle down.

(*PM* 398)

Various elements from the late lyrics we have looked at come together here, though they have a more florid setting that is familiar to readers of Stevens's evocations of Florida in his earlier work. At the risk of freezing the poem into a flat Oriental posture, let me paraphrase: at the end of the mind's imaginings, there is a palm and in the palm sits a bird that sings a foreign song that we do not understand. This song, like the cry of leaves, like the howling of the dove, is without human meaning and human feeling. Things merely *are:* the palm, the bird, its song, its feathers, the wind moving slowly in the branches. One can say no more. Stevens suggests that it is not human reason or even unreason that makes us happy, but something else, something foreign and real that we cannot even imagine, something that gives life as it is, that we live from and which is not the transfigurative sorcery of the imagination. As he observes in 'Note on Moonlight', what is at stake here is 'the mere objectiveness of things',

It is as if being was to be observed,
As if, among the possible purposes
Of what one sees, the purpose that comes first,
The surface, is the purpose to be seen.

(*CP* 531)

the thing itself and its seasons

Esse est percipi, the philosopher might mutter. Yet, as so often in Stevens, this thesis is wrapped in a conjectural 'as if' – and where would Stevens's poetry be without those two qualifying syllables?[6] What is perceived is the surface of things that are real but which resist our attempts to comprehend them. Our only acquaintance with things is with their surface, not their depths. This is a being which is mere, sheer fact, the simple 'there is' of things.

Skeletal existence

This concern with the thing itself, with mere being as it is, goes together with another feature of the late verse, the notion of life as an illusion and of having lived what Stevens calls 'a skeleton's life' (*PM* 395). This is not so much what we might call the Gnostical moment in Stevens's dark metaphysics, but rather the thought that the august activity of the imagination simply produces illusions when set against the hard, alien reality of the thing itself, what Stevens calls 'The Rock'. The poem begins,

> It is an illusion that we were ever alive,
> Lived in the houses of mothers, arranged ourselves
> By our own motions in a freedom of air.

> (*PM* 362)

The reality of mere being is without human purpose and human meaning. It is a skeletal existence that is linked, as I have already mentioned, to the fact of senescence, that these are the poems of an old man, written in what he calls 'a wakefulness inside a sleep'

(*PM* 370). Read in this light, it is difficult not to read a little auto-biographical self-reference into the wonderful late poem about Santayana, 'To an Old Philosopher in Rome'. The philosopher is described as 'dozing in the depths of wakefulness . . . alive yet living in two worlds' (*PM* 372), which is exactly the same formulation that describes the poet himself in 'An Old Man Asleep', 'The two worlds are asleep, are sleeping, now' (*PM* 382). The first part of 'The Rock' is called 'Seventy Years Later', and 'Long and sluggish lines' opens with,

> It makes so little difference, at so much more
> Than seventy, here one looks, one has been there before.
>
> (*PM* 370)

One has been here before. One hears the birds sing, but one has heard them before. One sees the trees and leaves, but one has seen them before,

> The trees have a look as if they bore sad names
> And kept saying over and over one same, same thing.
>
> (*PM* 370)

Life is empty repetition, as the Gnostic Strindberg counsels. The agèd poet is a skeleton, a talking, rattling bag of bones, what Stevens calls 'a naked egg'. As such, he begins to doubt himself and undo what he has done in his art. He writes, with savage self-reference and in allusion to 'The Man with the Blue Guitar',

the thing itself and its seasons

. . . The sounds of the guitar
Were not and are not. Absurd. The words spoken
Were not and are not. It is not to be believed.

(*PM* 362)

Stevens's self-undoing

The self-undoing of Stevens's art can be seen most acutely in a pair
of autobiographical poems, where the first is an earlier version of
the second: 'First Warmth' and 'As You Leave the Room'. The first
seems to date from 1947, the second appears to be one of the very
last poems Stevens wrote. It begins, once more, with the theme of
the skeleton,

I wonder, have I lived a skeleton's life,
As a questioner about reality,

A countryman of all the bones of the world?
Now, here, the warmth I had forgotten becomes

Part of major reality, part of
An appreciation of a reality;

And thus an elevation, as if I lived
With something I could touch, touch every way.

(*PM* 395)

These four short stanzas, despite their sombre mood and distinctly minor key, might be read as being consistent with Stevens's poetics, with their emphasis on warmth and elevation. But watch how these stanzas are subtly undone by four surrounding stanzas in the later version of the poem,

You speak. You say: Today's character is not
A skeleton out of its cabinet. Nor am I.

That poem about the pineapple, the one
About the mind as never satisfied,

The one about the credible hero, the one
About summer, are not what skeletons think about.

I wonder have I lived a skeleton's life,
As a disbeliever in reality,

A countryman of all the bones in the world?
Now, here, the snow I had forgotten becomes

Part of major reality, part of
An appreciation of a reality

And thus an elevation, as if I left
With something I could touch, touch every way.

the thing itself and its seasons

And yet nothing has been changed except what is
Unreal, as if nothing had been changed at all.

(PM 395–6)

These paired poems might be read in terms of a shift in Stevens's work. This is a turning away from the imaginative transfiguration of reality towards the hardness and plainness of reality itself. Philosophically speaking, it is a turn towards what I called above 'dejected transcendental idealism', where the poet testifies to a reality that escapes poetic evocation, making the whole activity of poetry appear futile: 'O Lady! We receive but what we give / And in our life alone does nature live.'

With this in mind, the alterations made to the second version of the poem are striking: the word 'questioner' is replaced with the stronger term 'disbeliever', the 'warmth' that was forgotten is directly inverted into 'snow', recalling 'The Snow Man' from 1921. The verb 'lived' in stanza four becomes 'left', suggesting a departure from life itself. Around these central stanzas, Stevens adds the conceit of another personage, who speaks to the poet about his work. This other voice states that the character of today, living in the reality of today, is not a skeleton, and neither is the poet who wrote Stevens's verse. There then follow a series of specific allusions to poems by Stevens from the 1940s: 'Someone Puts a Pineapple Together' (1947, *NA* 83–9), 'The Well Dressed Man with a Beard' (1941, *PM* 190), 'Examination of the Hero in the Time of War' (1942, *PM* 198–206), and 'Credences of Summer'(1947, *PM* 287–92). The other voice speaks words of consolation to the poet, but instead of finding reassurance, the poet begins to doubt, 'I wonder, have I lived a

79

skeleton's life?'. More interesting still is the final stanza, where the 'elevation' produced through the radiant atmosphere of the poet's *mundo* is quietly, but dramatically, qualified in another 'as if'. The only thing that poetry transforms is in itself unreal, simply the fictive doings of the imagination. Therefore, nothing has been changed, nothing has been touched by poetry. There is no elevation, no radiance, no warmth. As Bloom points out, perhaps Stevens is recalling Blake's declaration, in his last letter, that dying is no more than going out of one room and into another.[7] However, the whole mood of the second poem calls to mind Yeats's painfully honest very late poem, 'The Circus Animals' Desertion'. Here the poet looks back on his work and finds it utterly vain and delusory,

Players and painted stage took all my love,
And not those things that they were emblems of.

Yeats's hybristic mythologizing and self-mythologizing grew in what he calls 'pure mind', but began in ordinary things, 'old kettles, old bottles and a broken can', what he now calls 'a mound of refuse'. It is to this rubbish that Yeats, at the end of his career, is forced to return at the foot of the winding stair of the poet's tower,

Now that my ladder's gone,
I must lie down where all the ladders start,
In the foul rag-and-bone shop of the heart.[8]

Returning to 'As You Leave the Room', consider the allusion to 'The Well Dressed Man with a Beard'. The latter poem finishes

the thing itself and its seasons

with the line, 'It can never be satisfied, the mind, never'. This can be linked to a central motif of Stevens's poetry: the mind's desire will always exceed the beauty that poetry can bring to reality. In 'The Poems of Our Climate', Stevens asserts that the beauty of 'Clear water in a brilliant bowl' is not enough, 'One desires so much more than that' (*PM* 158). The pleasures of the static aesthetic image are always going to be transient, outrun by the desire that is their creative source. Words are chosen out of a desire that outstrips them (*PM* 318).[9] In comparison with that sentiment, the above poems would seem to exhibit desire's contraction. Desire is here less than the poem and the poem itself is nothing because it only effects a change in what is unreal and is hence no change at all. Poetry is powerless. It is powerlessness itself. A powerlessness which can at best dimly echo the passivity of things as they are given.

The métier of nothingness

Stevens is about as close as one can get to giving up verse in verse. Desire contracts, the mind empties, the floors of memory are wiped clean and nothingness flows over us without meaning. This is at its most extreme in the late lyric, 'A Clear Day and No Memories',

> No soldiers in the scenery,
> No thoughts of people now dead,
> As they were fifty years ago,
> Young and living in a live air,
> Young and walking in the sunshine,

Bending in blue dresses to touch something,
Today the mind is not part of the weather.

Today the air is clear of everything.
It has no knowledge except of nothingness
And it flows over us without meanings,
As if none of us had ever been here before
And are not now: in this shallow spectacle,
This invisible activity, this sense.

(*PM* 397)

Is this nothingness the threshold to Stoical contentment, secret wisdom or some Zen-like affirmation of the void? I see little evidence for that inference. On the contrary, the poet's vivid evocation of the past seems to conjure a deep sense of regret that is more than wistful, if less than despairing. We seem to be left with nothing, and, as we all know, nothing comes of nothing.

Yet this would be a mistake. For if Stevens seems close to giving up verse, then he does this *in verse*. As he puts it in 'The Rock', with yet another 'as if',

As if nothingness contained a métier,
A vital assumption, an impermanence
In its permanent cold, an illusion so desired

That the green leaves came and covered the high rock,
That the lilacs came and bloomed, like a blindness cleaned,
Exclaiming bright sight, as it was satisfied,

the thing itself and its seasons

In a birth of sight. The blooming and the musk
Were being alive, an incessant being alive,
A particular of being, that gross universe.

(*PM* 363)

The rock is the thing, a hard alien reality in the face of which the
soundings of the blue guitar become absurd. The rock is 'the gray
particular of man's life' (*PM* 364), and the environment of the poet
is permanent cold. Yet, Stevens insists, that nothingness contains
a métier, a work, a craft, a task. This task is the production of a
desired illusion, the green leaves that cover the rock, that bloom
into lilacs. If the rock is the thing, then the leaves are the poem,
the living particular of being. The leaves that cover the rock are
what Stevens calls the 'icon' of the poem, the beautiful illusion of a
fiction. Yet this is not enough; icons mean nothing if they contain
no grain or affluence of the reality they purport to describe. Stevens
insists, iconoclastically,

It is not enough to cover the rock with leaves.
We must be cured of it by a cure of the ground . . .

(*PM* 363)

What seems to be at stake in 'The Rock', and in many other of these
late lyrics, is the desire to be cured of the desire for poetry – which
returns to the theme of therapy and gives it an unexpected twist.
This is what Stevens means by 'a cure of the ground'. That is,
poetry can endlessly make 'meanings of the rock', but if these meanings are nothing when set against the rock, then they are worthless,

they are gaudy baubles. The cure, then, is the rock itself, 'the main of things'. In 'The Red Fern', a wonderful short lyric oddly not included in *The Palm at the End of the Mind*, this is what Stevens calls, 'the physical fix of things' (*CP* 365).[10] It is to this hard reality that the words of the poet must attend,

> It is the rock where tranquil must adduce
> Its tranquil self, the main of things, the mind,
> The starting point of the human and the end . . .
>
> (*PM* 365)

It is *as if* we had been brought to the end of the imagination, yet the end of the imagination had still to be imagined. It is with this weaker and more realist sense of the transfigurative powers of the imagination, in the face of a climate of coldness and a time of war, that poetry can be brought closer to the plain sense of things, to things in their remoteness from us and our intentions. Things merely are. As our long conversation with Stevens has shown, this simple truth is very difficult to say.

Conclusion

I love Maurice Blanchot.[1]

Are there two temptations in poetry, two philosophical poles that attract the poet first in one direction and then another? On the one hand, there is what we might call the idealist temptation premised on the belief that reality can be reduced to, and is indeed the product of, the imagination. We encountered this temptation with Stevens's talk of his intimidating thesis, the supreme fiction and the idea that the world is what you make of it, a world in words. On the other hand, there is the realist temptation that shows that poetry is concerned with the rubbings of a reality that resists the power of imagination, a reality that will always remain alien to the poet. In the preceding chapter, we outlined this poetry of hard reality, a poetry of the antipodes of poetry.

Stevens's poetry would seem to be divided, perhaps even torn, between these two temptations, between imagination reducing reality to itself and reality reducing the imagination's power to impotence. Stevens's verse seems to oscillate first one way and then the other, <u>between high summer and deep winter</u>, between ideas about the thing and the thing itself. This idea of poetic experience as an oscillation between idealism and realism recalls a central theme in the work of Maurice Blanchot, whom Stevens appears to have read through Blanchot's essays in the *Nouvelle Revue Française* and even 'loved'. For Blanchot, literature is divided between what he calls two slopes which represent two irresistible temptations for the writer.[2] On the one hand, literature is an act of idealization governed by the desire to assimilate all reality to the ego and to view the former as the latter's projection. This is a temptation that Blanchot associates with the odd couple Hegel and the Marquis de Sade, where absolute idealism is the rage of the belly turned mind and conceptuality is a means of cruel domination over things. When I name a thing, I both master it and kill it – which makes Adam the first serial killer. On the other hand, the second slope of literature does not aim to reduce reality to the imagination, but rather to let things be in their separateness from us. On this view, literature takes the side of things and tries to let things thing, as it were, to let substantives verbalize: letting the orange orange, the oyster oyster, the palm palm, and so on. Blanchot associates this view with the exquisite poetry of Francis Ponge, in particular his aptly titled, *Le parti pris des choses* (*Taking the Side of Things*) and Emmanuel Levinas's idea of what he calls the *il y a*, the sheer 'there is' of things where they seem to look at us rather than us looking at them.[3] On this second slope, literature is the ever-failing attempt to see things as they are, in their porosity and denseness, in their earthiness and mineral quality. Something very close to this is going on in Terrence Malick's concern with nature, as we will see below.

conclusion

Blanchot's point, which Stevens's poetry would seem to amplify, is that literature is not just divided between these two temptations; in fact, neither of these temptations can be resisted and both of them lead ineluctably to failure. Stevens can neither reduce reality to the imagination nor extend the imagination into reality. The supreme fiction, which would have been the place where Blanchot's first and second slopes merged into one *piste*, was never written. It remains a possibility, true, but so do the existence of fairies, life on Uranus and world peace. All that Stevens gives us is a detailed series of notes towards the supreme fiction, and a series of stipulations on its nature divided into the three sections of the poem: 'It must be abstract', 'It must change', 'It must give pleasure'. Hugely impressive as they are, these notes are just that, musical notes towards some colossal but unwritten symphony. All we have is the sketch of a score, which doesn't even make it into rehearsal.

Stevens's poetry fails. Maybe all modern poetry fails. And maybe this is the point. In my view, poetry written in the wake of romanticism is defined by an experience of hubris and failure, of hubris presaging failure. For example, at the moment of saying 'God is dead, therefore I am', it is utterly unclear in what the 'I am' consists. It is a mere leaf blown by the wind, a vapour, an ember, a bubble. The moment of the ego's assertion, in swelling up to fill a universe without God, is also the point at which it shrinks to insignificance. This is a lesson of which Nietzsche was acutely aware in his so-called autobiography, *Ecce Homo*, where ironically hubristic chapter titles like 'Why I am so clever' and 'Why I am a Destiny' simply serve to underline the chronic atrophy of the self. Yet failure contains an imperative, something which I think is suggested in Stevens's late lyrics, what I called above the métier of nothingness. Such a nothingness prescribes a task and requires a craft, namely the endless activity of description in the full awareness of failure. Failure is here defined by the courage to persist with failure. As Beckett would say, 'try again, fail again, fail better'.

If Stevens's poetics has two feet, imagination and reality, then one might imagine the imposing figure of Stevens shifting his weight from one foot to the other throughout his work, from summer to winter to somewhere in between. However, the movement that we have followed in his verse shows Stevens leaning decisively towards the poetry of reality. From his intimidating thesis on poetry as the imagination of life, we are led to a poetic antipoetry, an antipodes of poetry that rubs against the grain of the real that resists it. As he puts it in the *Adagia*, 'poetry increases the feeling for reality' (*OP* 188). The feeling that we feel for a real given to us through poetic experience is, I think, calm. We see things in their mereness, in their plainness and remoteness from us, and we accept it calmly, without the frustrated assertions and juvenile overreachings of the will. Such calm is not thoughtless, but rather thoughtful, the contemplative insight that comes from having things in sight. At its best, poetry offers an experience of the world as meditation, the mind slowing in front of things, the mind pushing back against the pressure of reality through the minimal transfigurations of the imagination. Such meditation, and this is crucial, does not shut its eyes to things, to the dark and bloody violence of the world, trying to imagine another world. Rather, those things are seen under a different aspect, subject to what I called in my opening propositions a felt variation, minimally but

conclusion

decisively transfigured. Poetry increases our feeling for reality by allowing us to see it, to focus on that which we normally pass over in our everyday activity: the world. By attending to the meditative voice of Stevens, I think we can acquire something of the craft of this calm, what he calls in German in the *Adagia*, 'Seelenfriede durch Dichtung' (*OP* 190), soul-peace through poetry. Or so we say.

Afterword

Calm – on Terrence Malick

Life contracts and death is expected,
As in a season of autumn.
The soldier falls.

He does not become a three-days personage,
Imposing his separation,
Calling for pomp.

Death is absolute and without memorial,
As in a season of autumn,
When the wind stops,

When the wind stops and, over the heavens,
The clouds go, nevertheless,
In their direction.

Wallace Stevens, 'The Death of a Soldier' (*PM* 35)

Wittgenstein asks a question, which sounds like the first line of a joke: How does one philosopher address another? To which the unfunny and perplexing riposte is, 'Take your time'.[1] Terrence Malick is evidently someone who takes his time. Since his first movie, *Badlands*, was premiered at the New York Film Festival in 1973, he has directed just two more: *Days of Heaven*, in 1979, and then nearly a twenty-year gap until the long-awaited 1998 movie, *The Thin Red Line*, which is the topic of this Afterword.

It is a war film. It deals with the events surrounding the battle for Guadalcanal in November 1942, as the US Army fought its bloody way north across the islands of the South Pacific against ferocious Japanese resistance. But it is a war film in the same way that Homer's *Iliad* is a war poem. The viewer seeking verisimilitude and documentation of historical fact will be disappointed. Malick's movie is a story of what we called above 'heroic fact': of death, of fate, of pointed and pointless sacrifice. Finally, it is a tale of love, both erotic love and, more importantly, the love of compassion whose cradle is military combat and whose greatest fear is dishonour. In one night-time scene, we see Captain Starros in close-up praying, 'Let me not betray my men'.

The ambition of *The Thin Red Line* is unapologetically epic, the scale is not historical but mythical, and the language is lyrical, even at times metaphysical. At one point in the film, Colonel Tall, the commanding officer of the campaign, cites a Homeric epithet about 'rosy-fingered dawn', and confesses to the Greek-American Starros that he read the *Iliad* in Greek whilst a student at West Point military academy – Starros himself speaks Greek on two occasions. Like the *Iliad*, Malick deals with the huge human themes by focus-

afterword

ing not on a whole war, and not even with an overview of a whole battle, but on the lives of a group of individuals – C-for-Charlie company – in a specific aspect of a battle over the period of a couple of weeks.

To non-Americans – and perhaps to many contemporary Americans as well – the significance of Guadalcanal might not be familiar. It was the key battle in the war against Japan, in a campaign that led from the attack on Pearl Harbor in 1941 to American victory and post-war imperial hegemony. If we cast the Japanese in the role of the Trojans, and Guadalcanal in the place of Troy, then *The Thin Red Line* might be said to recount the pre-history of American empire in the same way as Homer recites the pre-history of Hellenic supremacy. It might be viewed as a founding myth, and like all such myths, from Homer to Vergil to Milton, it shows both the necessity for an enemy in the act of founding and the often uncanny intimacy with that enemy. Some of the most haunting images of the film are those in which members of Charlie company sit face-to-face with captured Japanese soldiers surrounded by corpses, mud, and the dehumanizing detritus of battle.

Malick based his screenplay on James Jones's 500-page 1963 novel, *The Thin Red Line*.[2] Jones served as an infantryman in the US Army in the South Pacific, and *The Thin Red Line*, though fictional, is extensively based on Jones's wartime experiences. Jones was following the formula he established in his first book, the 900-page 1952 raw blockbuster, *From Here to Eternity*, which deals with events surrounding the bombing of Pearl Harbor.[3] A highly expurgated version of *From Here to Eternity*, starring Burt Lancaster, Deborah Kerr, Montgomery Clift and Frank Sinatra, won the Academy

Award for Best Motion Picture in 1953. Malick's movie won just one Oscar, to Hans Zimmer, for best original score.

A curious fact to note about Malick's *The Thin Red Line* is that it is a remake. Jones's book was turned into a movie directed by Andrew Marton and starring Keir Dullea and Jack Warden in 1964. This is a low budget, technically clumsy, averagely acted, and indeed slightly saucy movie, where the jungles of the South Pacific have been replanted in Spain, where the picture was shot. But it is a good, honest picture, and there are many analogues with Malick's version, particularly the dialogues between Colonel Tall and Captain Stein.

The narrative focus of the 1964 picture is on Private Doll, who is an independently minded existentialist rebel, closer to a young Brando than to Albert Camus, who discovers himself in the heat of battle through killing 'Japs'. The guiding theme is the insanity of war, the thin red line between the sane and the mad, and we are offered a series of more or less trite reflections on the meaningless-ness of war. Yet, in this respect, the 1964 film is much more faithful to James Jones's 1963 novel than Malick's treatment, with its more metaphysical intimations. In the 1964 movie, the existential hero finds himself through the act of killing. War is radical meaningless-ness, but it is that in relation to which meaning can be given to an individual life. Doll eventually crosses the thin red line and goes crazy, killing everyone in sight, including his own comrades.

The novel is a piece of tough-minded and earnest Americana, somewhere between fiction and reportage that at times brilliantly evokes the exhausting and dehumanizing pointlessness of war. The book's great virtue is its evocation of camaraderie, the physical and emotional intensity of the relations between the men in C-for-

Charlie company. Some of the characters are finely and fully drawn, in particular Fife, Doll and Bell, but I don't think it is too severe to say that James Jones is not James Joyce. Yet, in this regard, the novel serves Malick's purposes extremely well because it provides him with the raw narrative prime matter from which to form his screenplay. For example, the central protagonist of Malick's version, Witt, brilliantly played by Jim Caviezel, is a more marginal figure in Jones's novel. He drifts repeatedly in and out of the action, having been transferred from Charlie company to Cannon Company, which is a collection of brigands and reprobates, but he is eventually readmitted to Charlie company because of his exceptional valour in battle. He is depicted as a stubborn, single-minded, half-educated troublemaker from Breathitt County, Kentucky, motivated by racism, a powerful devotion to his comrades, and an obscure ideal of honour. Although there is an essential solitude to Witt's character that must have appealed to Malick, the latter transforms him into a much more angelic, self-questioning, philosophical figure. Indeed, the culminating action of Malick's film is Witt's death, which does not even occur in the novel, where he is shown at the end of the book finally reconciled with Fife, his former buddy. Fife is the central driving character of Jones's novel, together with Doll, Bell and Welsh. I have been informed that Malick shot about seven hours of film, but had to cut it to three hours to meet his contract. Therefore, the whole story of Fife – and doubtless much else – was cut out. Other of Malick's characters are inventions, like Captain Starros, the Greek who takes the place of the Jewish Captain Stein. And, interestingly, there are themes in the novel that Malick does not take up, such as the homosexual relations between comrades, in particular Doll's emerging acknowledgement that he is gay.

It would appear that Malick has a very free relation to his material. But appearances can be deceptive. For Jones, there was a clear thematic and historical continuity between *From Here to Eternity* and *The Thin Red Line*, and Malick respects that continuity by integrating passages and characters from the former book into his screenplay. For example, the character of Colonel Tall is lifted from the earlier novel and, more importantly, Prewitt in *From Here To Eternity* becomes fused with Witt, becoming literally pre-Witt. As Jimmie E. Cain has shown in an invaluable article, Prewitt's speculations about his mother's death and the question of immortality are spoken by Witt in the important opening scenes of *The Thin Red Line*. After Malick had repeatedly consulted Gloria Jones, the late novelist's wife, about the slightest changes from novel to screenplay, she apparently remarked, 'Terry, you have my husband's voice, you're writing in his musical key; now what you must do is improvise. Play riffs on this.'[4]

Malick crafts the matter of Jones's work into a lyrical, economical and highly wrought screenplay. Whilst there are many memorable passages of dialogue, and some extraordinarily photographed extended action sequences, the core of the film is carried by Malick's favourite cinematic technique, the voiceover. This is worth considering in some detail. As Michael Filippidis has argued, the voiceover provides the entry point for all three of Malick's films.[5] In *Badlands*, the voiceovers are provided by Holly (Sissy Spacek), and in *Days of Heaven* by the child Linda (Linda Manz). The technique of the voiceover allows the character to assume a distance from the cinematic action and a complicity with the audience, an intimate

afterword

distance that is meditative, ruminative, at times speculative. It is like watching a movie with someone whispering into your ear.

If the technique of the voiceover is common to all three films, then what changes in *The Thin Red Line* is the subject of the narration. *Badlands* and *Days of Heaven* are narrated from a female perspective and it is through the eyes of two young, poorly educated women that we are invited to view the world. In *The Thin Red Line*, the voiceovers are male and plural. The only female characters are the wife of Bell who appears in dream sequences and whose only words are 'Come out. Come out where I am', the young Melanesian mother that Witt meets at the beginning of the film, and the recollected scene of Witt's mother's death-bed. Although it is usually possible to identify the speaker of the voiceover, their voices sometimes seem to blend into one another, particularly during the closing scenes of the film when the soldiers are leaving Guadalcanal on board a landing craft. As the camera roams from face to face, almost drunkenly, the voices become one voice, one soul, 'as if all men got one big soul' – but we will come back to this.

The Thin Red Line is words with music. The powerful effect of the voiceovers cannot be distinguished from that of the music which accompanies them. The score, which merits sustained listening on its own account, was composed by Hans Zimmer, who collaborated extensively with Malick. The use of music in Malick's movies is at times breathtaking, and the structure of his films bears a close relation to musical composition, where leitmotifs function as both punctuation and recapitulation of the action – a technique Malick employed to great effect in *Days of Heaven*. In all three of his movies, there is a persistent presence of natural sounds, particularly flowing water and birdsong. The sound of the breeze in the vast fields of ripening wheat in *Days of Heaven* finds a visual echo in what was the most powerful memory I had from my first viewing of *The Thin Red Line*: the sound of the wind and soldiers' bodies moving through the Kunai grass as Charlie company ascend the hill towards the enemy position. Nature appears as an impassive and constant presence that frames human conflict.

Three hermeneutic banana skins

There are a number of hermeneutic banana skins that any study of Malick's art can slip up on, particularly when the critic professes to be a philosopher. Before turning more directly to the film, let me take my time to discuss three of them.

First, there is what we might call the paradox of privacy. Malick is clearly a very private person who shuns publicity. This is obviously no easy matter in the movie business and in this regard Malick invites comparison with Kubrick who, by contrast, appears a paragon of productivity. Of course, the relative paucity of biographical data on Malick simply feeds a curiosity of the most trivial and quotidian kind. I must confess to this curiosity myself, but I do not think it should be sated. There should be no speculation, then, on 'the enigmatic Mr Malick', or whatever.

But if one restricts oneself to the biographical information that I have been able to find out, then a second banana skin appears in one's path, namely the intriguing issue of Malick and philosophy. He studied philosophy at Harvard University between 1961 and

1965, graduating with Phi Beta Kappa honours. He worked closely with Stanley Cavell, who supervised Malick's undergraduate honors thesis. Against the deeply ingrained prejudices about Continental thought that prevailed at that time, Malick courageously attempted to show how Heidegger's thoughts about (and against) epistemology in *Being and Time* could be seen in relation to the analysis of perception in Russell, Moore and, at Harvard, C.I. Lewis. Malick then went, as a Rhodes Scholar, to Magdalen College, Oxford, to study for the BPhil in philosophy. He left Oxford because he wanted to write a DPhil thesis on the concept of world in Kierkegaard, Heidegger and Wittgenstein, and was told by Gilbert Ryle that he should try to write on something more 'philosophical'. He then worked as a philosophy teacher at MIT, teaching Hubert Dreyfus's course on Heidegger when Dreyfus was away on study leave in France, and wrote journalism for the *New Yorker* and *Life* magazine. In 1969, he published his bilingual edition of Heidegger's *Vom Wesen des Grundes* as *The Essence of Reasons*.[6] Also in 1969 he was accepted into the inaugural class of the Center for Advanced Film Studies at the American Film Institute, in Los Angeles, and his career in cinema began to take shape.

Clearly, then, Malick's is a highly sophisticated, philosophically trained intellect. Yet the young philosopher decided not to pursue an academic career, but to pass from philosophy to film, for reasons that remain obscure. Given these facts, it is extremely tempting – almost overwhelmingly so – to read through his films to some philosophical pre-text or meta-text, to interpret the action of his characters in Heideggerian, Wittgensteinian or, indeed, Cavellian terms. To make matters worse, Malick's movies seem to make philosophical statements and present philosophical positions. None-theless, to read through the cinematic image to some identifiable philosophical master text would be a mistake, for it would be not to read at all.

So, what is the professional philosopher to do when faced with Malick's films? This leads me to a third hermeneutic banana skin. To read from cinematic language to some philosophical metalanguage is both to miss what is specific to the medium of film and usually to engage in some sort of cod-philosophy deliberately designed to intimidate the uninitiated. I think this move has to be avoided on philosophical grounds, indeed the very best Heideggerian grounds. Any philosophical reading of film has to be a reading *of* film, of what Heidegger would call *der Sache selbst*, the thing itself. A philo-sophical reading of film should not be concerned with ideas about the thing, but with the thing itself, the cinematic *Sache*. It seems to me that a consideration of Malick's art demands that we take seriously the idea that film is less an illustration of philosophical ideas and theories – let's call that a *philoso-fugal* reading – than a form of philosophizing, of reflection, reasoning and argument.[7]

Loyalty, love, and truth

Let me now turn to the film itself. The narrative of *The Thin Red Line* is organized around three relationships, each composed of a con-flict between two characters. The first relationship is between Colonel Tall, played by Nick Nolte, and Captain Starros, played by Elias Koteas. At the core of this relationship is the question of loyalty, a conflict between loyalty to the commands of one's superiors and loyalty to the men under one's command. This relationship comes to a crisis when Starros refuses a direct order from Tall to lead an attack on a machine gun position of the Japanese. Starros says that 'I've lived with these men for two and a half years, and I will not order them to their deaths' – for the carnage that the Japanese are causing from their superior hill-top vantage point and the scenes of slaughter are truly awful. Suppressing his fury, Tall goes up the line to join Charlie company and skilfully organizes a flanking assault on the Japanese position. After the successful assault, he gives Starros a humiliating lecture about the necessity of allowing one's men to die in battle. He decides that Starros is not tough-minded enough to lead his men and, after recommending him for the Silver Star and the Purple Heart, immediately relieves him of his commission and orders him back to a desk job in Washington D.C. Loyalty to the men under one's command must be subservient to the pragmatics of the battlefield.

The second relationship, based on love, is between Private Bell (Ben Chaplin), and his wife Marty (Miranda Otto), and is dealt with rather abstractly by Malick. It is much more central to the 1964 version of the film, where it is transposed into the relationship between Private Doll and one 'Judy'. In Jones's novel, Bell is a former army officer who had been a First Lieutenant in the Philippines. He and his wife had an extraordinarily close, intense relationship ('We were always very sexual together', he confesses to Fife), and after spending four months separated from his wife in the jungle, he decided that he'd had enough and resigned his commission. As retribution, the US Army said that they would make sure he was drafted into the infantry as a private. All that we see of the relationship in the film is a series of dream images of Bell with Marty, what Jones calls 'weird transcendental images of Marty's presence'. Then, after the battle, we hear Bell reading a letter from his wife saying that she has left him for an Air Force captain.

After the failures of loyalty and love, the theme of truth is treated in the third relationship, and this is what I would like to concentrate on. The characters are Sergeant Welsh, played with consummate craft by Sean Penn, and Private Witt. The question at issue here is metaphysical truth; or, more precisely, whether there is such a thing as metaphysical truth. Baldly stated: is this the only world, or is there another world? The conflict is established in the first dialogue between the two soldiers, after Witt has been incarcerated for going AWOL in a Melanesian village, in the scenes of somewhat cloying communal harmony that open the film. Welsh says, 'in this world, a man himself is nothing . . . and there ain't no world but this one'. To which Witt replies, 'You're wrong there, I seen another world. Sometimes I think it's just my imagination.' Welsh completes the thought: 'Well, you're seeing something I never will.'

Welsh is a sort of physicalist egoist who is contemptuous of everything. Jones writes,

> Everything amused Welsh . . . Politics amused him, religion amused him, particularly ideals and integrity amused him; but most of all human virtue amused him. He did not believe in it and did not believe in any of those other words.
>
> (p. 24)

Behind this complete moral nihilism, the only thing in which Welsh believes is property. He refuses to let Starros commend him for a Silver Star after an act of extraordinary valour in which he dodged hails of bullets to give morphine to a buddy dying on the battle-field, and quips, 'Property, the whole fucking thing's about property'. War is fought for property, one nation against another nation. The war is taking place in service of a lie, the lie of prop-erty. You either believe the lie or you die, like Witt. Welsh says – and it is a sentiment emphasized in the book and both versions of the film – 'Everything is a lie. Only one thing a man can do, find something that's his, make an island for himself.' It is only by believ-ing that, and shutting his eyes to the bloody lie of war, that he can survive. Welsh's physicalism is summarized in the phrase that in many ways guides the 1964 version of the film and which appears briefly in Malick: 'It's only meat.' The human being is meat and only this belief both exposes the lie and allows one to survive – and Welsh survives.

Facing Welsh's nihilistic physicalism is what we might call Witt's Emersonian metaphysical panpsychism, caught in the question, 'Maybe all men got one big soul that everybody's a part of – all faces are the same man, one big self.' Witt is the questioner, the contemplator, the mystic, perhaps even the holy fool. Much of what he says is in the form of questions – the very piety of think-ing for Heidegger – and not the assertions propounded by Welsh. Unflinchingly brave in combat, with absolutely no thought of his own safety and prepared to sacrifice himself for his comrades, Witt views all things and persons with an impassive constancy, and sees beauty and goodness in all things. Where Welsh sees only the pain caused by human selfishness, Witt looks at the same scenes and feels the glory. He is like a redemptive angel looking into the souls of soldiers and seizing hold of their spark. It is this metaphysical commitment which fuels both Witt's selfless courage in combat and his compassion for the enemy. In one of the most moving scenes of the film, he looks into the face of a dead Japanese soldier, half-buried in the dirt – which speaks to him with a prophecy of his own fate – 'Are you loved by all? Know that I was. Do you imagine that your sufferings will be less because you loved goodness, truth?' In their final dialogue, Witt says that he still sees a spark in Sergeant Welsh. The truth is, I think, that Welsh is half in love with Witt, and behind his nihilism there is a grudging but total respect for Witt's commitment. Welsh cannot believe what Witt believes, he cannot behold the glory. And yet, he is also unable to feel nothing, to feel numb to the suffering that surrounds him. As a consequence, he is in profound pain. In tears, at the foot of Witt's grave, Welsh asks, 'Where's your spark now?', which might as well be a question to himself.

As in the two other relationships, there seems to be a clear winner and loser. As Welsh predicts in their second dialogue, the reward for Witt's metaphysical commitment will be death. Loyalty to one's men leads to dismissal from one's position, loyalty in love leads to betrayal, and loyalty to a truth greater than oneself leads to death. Yet Malick is too intelligent to make didactic art. Truth consists in the conflict, or series of conflicts, between positions; and in watching those conflicts unravel, we are instructed, deepened. This conflict is particularly clear in the depiction of war itself. For this is not simply an anti-war film and has none of the post-adolescent bombast of Francis Ford Coppola's *Apocalypse Now* (1979), the cloying self-righteousness of Oliver Stone's *Platoon* (1986), or the gnawing, sentimental nationalism of *Saving Private Ryan* (1998). One of the voiceovers states, 'Wars don't ennoble men. It turns them into dogs. Poisons the soul.' But this view has to be balanced with a central message of the film: namely, that there is a total risk of the self in battle, an utter emptying of the self that does not produce egoism, but rather a powerful bond of compassionate love for one's comrades and even for one's enemy. The inhumanity of war lets one see through the fictions of a people, a tribe or a nation towards a common humanity. The imponderable question is why it should require such suffering to bring us to this recognition.

Immortality

I would like to stay a little longer with the character of Witt and consider in detail one scene from the movie, namely the instant of his death. Witt, like all the male protagonists from Malick's previous movies, goes to his death with a sense of acceptance, willingness even. In *Badlands*, Kit (Martin Sheen), desires nothing more than the glorious notoriety of death and we assume at the end of the picture that he is going to be electrocuted. In *Days of Heaven*, the Farmer (Sam Shepherd) is told by his doctor that he is going to die, and it is this overheard conversation that prompts Bill (Richard Gere), into planning the deception of a marriage with his partner, Abby (Brooke Adams). After Gere stabs Shepherd to death in a smouldering wheat field, one has the sense that this is exactly what the Farmer desired. Similarly, when Bill is gunned down at the end of

Days of Heaven – in an amazing shot photographed from underwater as his face hits the river – one has a powerful intimation of an ineluctable fate working itself out. In short, Malick's male protagonists seem to foresee their appointment with death and endeavour to make sure they arrive on time. Defined by a fatalistic presentiment of their demise, they are all somehow in love with death. Yet such foreknowledge does not provoke fear and trembling; on the contrary, it brings, I will suggest, a kind of *calm*.

There is an utter recklessness to Witt and he repeatedly puts himself in situations of extreme danger. He is amongst the first to volunteer for the small unit that makes the highly dangerous flanking move to destroy the Japanese machine gun position, and the action that leads to his eventual death at the end of the film is very much of his own making. So, Witt fits the death-bound pattern of Malick's male protagonists. Yet what is distinctive about the character of Witt is that at the core of his sense of mortality lies the metaphysical question of immortality. This is established in the opening scenes of the movie in the Melanesian village, when he is shown talking to an unnamed comrade who has also gone AWOL. Against the recollected image of his mother's death-bed, he says,

> I remember my mother when she was dying, all shrunken and grey. I asked if she was afraid. She just shook her head. I was afraid to touch the death that I seen in her. I couldn't find anything beautiful or uplifting about her going back to God. I heard people talk about immortality, but I ain't never seen it.

afterword

The point here is that Witt is afraid of the death that descends over his mother; he can't touch it, find any comfort in it, or believe that it is the passage to her immortal home in bliss. Witt is then profiled standing on the beach, and he continues, less sceptically, and this time in a voiceover,

I wondered how it'd be when I died. What it'd be like to know that this breath now was the last one you was ever gonna draw. I just hope I can meet it the same way she did, with the same . . . calm. Because that's where it's hidden, the immortality that I hadn't seen.

It is this pause between 'same' and 'calm' that I want to focus on, this breathing space for a last breath. For I think this calm is the key to the film and, more widely, to Malick's art. The metaphysical issue of the reality or otherwise of immortality obviously cannot be settled and that is not the point. The thought here is that the only immortality imaginable is found in a calm that can descend at the moment of death. The eternal life can only be imagined as inhabiting the instant of one's death, of knowing that this is the last breath that you are going to draw and not being afraid.[8]

With this in mind, let's look at the instant of Witt's death. Charlie Company are making their way, very precariously, up a river, and the whole scene, as elsewhere in Malick, is saturated with the sound of flowing river water. Phone lines back to HQ have been cut; enemy artillery fire is falling all around them and is getting steadily closer. The company is under the command of the peculiarly incompetent Lieutenant Band, who is leading them into an extremely exposed position where they will be sitting ducks for an enemy attack. Rather than retreat, as he should have done, Bard hurriedly decides to send a small scouting party up the river to judge the proximity of the enemy. He chooses the terrified Fife and the adolescent Coombs, and then Witt quickly volunteers himself. After progressing a little way up the river, they are seen by the enemy and Coombs is shot, but not fatally wounded. Witt sends Fife back to the company and the wounded Coombs floats back downstream. In an act of complete selflessness, Witt allows himself to be used as a decoy and leads a squad of Japanese soldiers into the jungle. Witt then suddenly finds himself in a small clearing surrounded on all sides by some twenty Japanese troops. Breathless and motionless, he stands still whilst the Japanese squad leader screams at him, presumably demanding that he defend himself. Witt remains stock still, recovers his breath and then realizes that he is going to die. The scene seems agonizingly long, the music slowly builds and there is a slow zoom into Witt's face. He is . . . calm. Then the camera slowly zooms out and there is a brief cutting shot of him half-heartedly raising his gun as he is gunned down. Malick then cuts to images of nature, of trees, water and birds.

What is one to make of this? Obvious philosophical parallels can be drawn here. For example, Heidegger's notion of *Angst* or anxiety is experienced with the presentiment of my mortality, what he calls *being-towards-death*. In one famous passage from the 1929 lecture, 'What is Metaphysics?', a text that Malick surely knows as it is directly contemporary with *The Essence of Reasons*, Heidegger is anxious to distinguish *Angst* from all sorts of fear and trembling. He says that the experience of *Angst* is a kind of *Ruhe*, peace or calm.[9]

afterword

Similarly, in Blanchot's tantalizingly brief memoir, *L'instant de ma mort*, the seemingly autobiographical protagonist is described as being at the point of execution by German soldiers, a fate from which he eventually escapes. He describes the feeling as 'un sentiment de légèreté extraordinaire, une sorte de béatitude'.[10] One also thinks of Wittgenstein's remark from the *Tractatus*, 'If we take eternity to mean not infinite temporal duration but timelessness, then eternal life belongs to those who live in the present'.[11] One could go on amassing examples. To interpret Malick's treatment of death in line with such thoughts is extremely tempting, but it would be to slip up on one or more of those hermeneutic banana skins discussed above. It would be to offer ideas about the thing rather than *die Sache Selbst*.

At the core of *The Thin Red Line*, then, is this experience of calm in the face of death, of a kind of peace at the moment of one's extinction that is the only place one may speak of immortality. This experience of calm frames the film and paradoxically provides the context for the bloody and cruel action of war. In particular, it frames the character of Welsh, who cares for Witt and his 'beautiful light' much more than he can admit, but persists to the end of the film in his belief that everything is a lie. His final words are, 'You're in a box, a moving box. They want you dead or in their lie'.

All things shining – the place of nature in Malick

Why do I claim that calm is the key to Malick's art? To try and tease this out, I would like to turn to the theme of nature, whose massive presence is the constant backdrop to Malick's movies. If calm in the face of mortality is the frame for the human drama of

The Thin Red Line, then nature is the frame for this frame, a power that at times completely overshadows the human drama.

The Thin Red Line opens with the image of a huge crocodile slowly submerging into a weed-covered pond – the crocodile that makes a brief return appearance towards the end of the film, when he is shown captured by some men from Charlie Company, who prod it abstractedly with a stick. Against images of jungle trees densely wrapped in suffocating vines, we hear the first words of the movie, spoken by an unidentified voice,

> What's this war in the heart of nature? Why does nature vie with itself, the land contends with the sea? Is there an avenging power in nature? Not one power, but two.

Obviously, the war in the heart of nature has a double meaning, suggesting both a war internal to nature, and the human war that is being fought out amid such immense natural beauty. These two meanings are brought together later in the film by Colonel Tall, when he is in the process of dismissing Starros from his commission and justifying the brutality of war,

> Look at this jungle; look at those vines, the way they twine around the tress, swallowing everything. Nature is cruel, Starros.

Images of trees wrapped in vines punctuate *The Thin Red Line*, together with countless images of birds, in particular owls and parrots. These images are combined with the almost constant presence of natural sounds, of birdsong, of the wind in the Kunai grass, of animals moving in the undergrowth and the sound of water, both waves lapping on the beach and the flowing of the river.

Nature might be viewed as a kind of *fatum* for Malick, an ineluctable power, a warring force that both frames human war but is utterly indifferent to human purposes and intentions. This beautiful indifference of nature can be linked to the depiction of nature elsewhere in Malick's work. For example, *Badlands* is teeming with natural sounds and images: with birds, dogs, flowing water, the vast flatness of South Dakota and the badlands of Montana, with its mountains in the distance – and always remaining in the distance. *Days of Heaven* is also heavily marked with natural sounds and exquisitely photographed images, with flowing river water, the wind moving in fields of ripening wheat and silhouetted human figures working in vast fields. Nature possesses here an avenging power, when a plague of locusts descend on the fields and Sam Shepherd sets fire to his entire wheat-crop – nature is indeed cruel.

Although it is difficult not to grant that nature is playing a symbolic role for Malick, his is not an animistic conception of nature, of the kind that one finds lamented in Coleridge's 1802 'Dejection: An Ode' discussed above. In my opinion, nature's indifference to human purposes follows from a broadly naturalistic conception of nature. Things are not enchanted in Malick's universe, they simply *are*, and we are things too. They are remote from us and continue on regardless of our strivings. This is what is suggested by the Wallace Stevens poem cited in epigraph to this essay. A soldier falls in battle, but his death does not invite pomp or transient glory. Rather, death has an absolute character, which Stevens likens to a moment in autumn when the wind stops. Yet, when the wind stops, above in the high heavens the clouds continue on their course, 'nevertheless, / In their direction'. What is central to Malick, I think, is this 'nevertheless\ness' of nature, the fact that human death is absorbed into the relentlessness of nature, the eternal war in nature into which the death of a soldier is indifferently ingested. That's where Witt's spark lies.

There is a calm at the heart of Malick's art, a calmness to his cinematic eye, a calmness that is also communicated by his films, that becomes the mood of his audience. After watching *The Thin Red Line*, we feel calm. As Charlie Company leave Guadalcanal and are taken back to their ship on a landing craft, we hear the final voiceover from Witt, this time from beyond the grave,

> Oh my soul let me be in you now. Look out through my eyes, look out at the things you made, all things shining.

In each of his movies, one has the sense of things simply being looked at, just being what they are – trees, water, birds, dogs, crocodiles or whatever. Things simply are, and are not moulded to a human purpose. We watch things shining calmly, being as they are, in all the intricate evasions of 'as'. The camera can be pointed at those things to try and capture some grain or affluence of their reality. The closing shot of *The Thin Red Line*, reproduced on the cover of this book, presents the viewer with a coconut fallen onto the beach, against which a little water laps and out of which has sprouted a long green shoot, connoting life, one imagines. The coconut simply is, it merely lies there remote from us and our

afterword

intentions. This suggests to me Stevens's final poem, 'The Palm at the End of the Mind', the palm that simply persists regardless of the makings of 'human meaning'. Stevens concludes, 'The palm stands on the edge of space. The wind moves slowly in its branches'. In my fancy at least, I see Malick concurring with this sentiment.

Thanks

I have given talks on Wallace Stevens on several occasions, stretching back to an invitation from Chrisopher Hookway to speak to the Aristotelian Society in London in 1996.[1] Though I cannot mention all the people who have helped me to clarify and alter my thinking about Stevens, I am particularly indebted to: Gerald Bruns, Sebastian Gardner, Jay Bernstein, Josh Cohen, Edward Ragg, J. Hillis Miller, Andrew Gibson, Steven Connor, Gabriela Basterra, Jon Cook, Laura Hopkins and Tom McCarthy. I'd particularly like to thank Angela Livingstone for her thoughtful comments on parts of this book, for an epigraph, and for introducing me to Pasternak, a couple of whose words are littered in these pages. I would like to thank Pietra Palozzolo for bibliographical help and for her insights into Stevens's verse. Some of the occasions upon which I have spoken about Stevens stand out in my memory because they caused me to rethink my approach. I presented a French version of this argument at the Collège International de Philosophie in Paris in

November 2001 and I learnt much from discussions with Judith Balso and Alain Badiou. A compressed version of the early chapters was presented to the 'Philosophy As' conference at Senate House, University of London in November 2002, organized by Havi Carel and David Gamez. Thanks to Haim Luski and Lyat Friedman, I was allowed to share my interests in poetry over wine and food with a reading of various poems in Tel Aviv in April 2003. Particularly memorable, thanks to Rai Gaita, was a session on Stevens at the Australian Catholic University as part of the 2003 Simone Weil Lectures, where I gained much from an extremely engaged audience and from ensuing correspondence with Chris Wallace-Crabbe and others. A presentation to the American Studies seminar in Cambridge in November 2003 was very helpful in distilling my thoughts. Finally, the entirety of the Stevens text was presented in three lectures at the University of Essex in June 2004 and I'd like to thank colleagues and students for their questions: especially Mark Sacks, Tom Sorell, Beatrice Han, Fiona Hughes, Mike Weston, James Corby, Sharon Krishek, Clive Zammit and Giovanni Levi. The text on Malick originates in an invitation from Dominic Willsdon to introduce a screening of the movie at the Tate Modern in May 2002. I'd like to thank Keith Ansell-Pearson, Nick Bunnin, Stanley Cavell, Jim Conant, Hubert Dreyfus, Espen Hammer, Jim Hopkins, John Gibson, Robert Lang and Anne Latto for confirming and providing facts about Malick and also for helpful comments on my line of argument. Finally, I'd like to thank Daniel Morris for his invaluable help in preparing this book for publication.

thanks

Notes

2 *Poetry, philosophy and life as it is*

1 Helen Vendler, 'The Qualified Assertions of Wallace Stevens', in *The Act of the Mind: Essays on the Poetry of Wallace Stevens*, edited by R.H. Pearce and J. Hillis Miller (Johns Hopkins University Press, Baltimore, Md., 1965), p. 145.

2 On this fascinating topic, take a look at 'Wallace Stevens' Alleged Deathbed Conversion', www.english.upenn.edu/~afilreis/Stevens/conversion.html.

3 For a book-length account of Stevens and law, with particular emphasis on the implications of his poetry for the practice of law, see Thomas Grey, *The Wallace Stevens Case* (Harvard University Press, Cambridge, Mass., 1991).

4 *Critique of Pure Reason*, A371.

5 Hegel, *Introductory Lectures on Aesthetics*, trans. B. Bosanquet (Penguin, Harmondsworth, 1993), p. 4.

6 Friedrich Schlegel, *Philosophical Fragments*, trans. Peter Firchow (University of Minnesota Press, Minneapolis, 1991), p. 70.

7 Coleridge, *Poems*, ed. J. Beer (Dent, London, 1974), p. 281. I'd like to thank Jon Cook for reminding me of this passage from Coleridge.

8 See Sebastian Gardner, 'Wallace Stevens and Metaphysics: The Plain Sense of Things', in *European Journal of Philosophy*, 2: 3 (1994), pp. 322–44.

9 Harold Bloom, *Wallace Stevens: The Poems of Our Climate* (Cornell University Press, Ithaca, 1976); and Joseph Riddel, *The Clairvoyant Eye: The Poetry and Poetics of Wallace Stevens* (Louisiana State University Press, Baton Rouge, 1967).

10 See *The Clairvoyant Eye*, op. cit. p. 15.

11 See 'Metaphoric Staging: Stevens' Beginning Again of the "End of the Book"', in *Wallace Stevens: A Celebration*, eds Frank A. Doggett and Robert Buttel (Princeton University Press, Princeton, N.J., 1980), pp. 308–38.

12 Ibid., p. 335.

13 See *Wallace Stevens: The Poems of Our Climate*, op. cit. pp. 92–105.

14 Hilary Putnam, *Realism with a Human Face* (Harvard University Press, Cambridge, Mass., 1990).

15 Kant, *Critique of Pure Reason*, B103.

16 See *Being and Time*, trans. J. Macquarrie and E. Robinson (Blackwell, Oxford, 1962), pp. 244–56.

17 *OP* 192. For an interesting Heidegger-inspired reading of Stevens, see Gerald Bruns 'Stevens Without Epistemology', in *Wallace Stevens and the Poetics of Modernism*, op. cit. pp. 24–40.

18 Stevens dabbled – but no more than that – in phenomenology. Some evidence of this can be seen in the passing reference to Husserl in the 1951 lecture, 'A Collect of Philosophy', although Stevens is merely citing his correspondence with Jean Wahl (*OP* 275).

19 Merleau-Ponty, *Phenomenology of Perception*, trans. Colin Smith (Routledge, London, 1962), p. xix.

20 Charles Taylor, 'Overcoming Epistemology' in *After Philosophy: End or Transformation?* eds K. Baynes, J. Bohman and T. McCarthy (MIT Press, Cambridge, Mass., 1987), p. 477.

21 For an analogous critique of the idea that poetry makes knowledge

claims, where poetry is seen as a complex form of semantic embeddedness that requires historical, biographical and political understanding, see Raymond Geuss, 'Poetry and Knowledge', *Arion*, II: i (spring/summer 2003), pp. 1–31.

22 Frank Kermode, *Wallace Stevens* (Faber, London, 1960).

3 *Sudden rightnesses*

1 Friedrich Schlegel, *Philosophical Fragments*, op. cit. p. 21.

2 J. Hillis Miller, 'Wallace Stevens' Poetry of Being', *The Act of the Mind: Essays on the Poetry of Wallace Stevens*, edited by R.H. Pearce and J. Hillis Miller (Johns Hopkins University Press, Baltimore, Md., 1965), p. 145.

3 David Hockney, *The Blue Guitar* (Petersburg Press, London and New York, 1977).

4 For a good example of such an interpretation, see John Hollander, 'The Sound of the Music of Music and Sound', in *Wallace Stevens: A Celebration*, op. cit. pp. 235–55.

5 Interestingly, these words are cited as an epigraph to Jerry Fodor's critique of certain claims made for the computational theory of mind in *The Mind Doesn't Work That Way* (MIT Press, Cambridge, Mass., 2001).

6 Adorno, *Negative Dialektik* (Suhrkamp, Frankfurt a.M., 1966), p. 364.

7 Emerson, *Selected Essays*, ed. L. Ziff (Penguin, London, 1982), p. 100. The presence of this Emersonian inheritance in Stevens is one of the main contentions of Bloom's *Wallace Stevens: The Poems of our Climate*, op. cit.

8 On this theme, see the interesting essay by Roy Harvey Pearce, 'Towards Decreation: Stevens and the Theory of Poetry', in *Wallace Stevens: A Celebration*, op. cit. pp. 269–308.

4 *Wallace Stevens's intimidating thesis*

1   Hölderlin, 'Brod und Wein', in *Poems and Fragments*, trans. M. Hamburger (Cambridge University Press, Cambridge, 1980), p. 250. Heidegger's 'Wozu Dichter?', originally from 1946, can be found in *Holzwege* (Klostermann, Frankfurt am Main, 1980 [6th edition]), pp. 265–316.

5 *The twofold task of poetry*

1   As some commentators have pointed out, Stevens writes a poetry of notes. See Krzysztof Ziarek, 'The Other Notation. Stevens and the Supreme Fiction of Poetry', in *Inflected Language: Toward a Hermeneutic of Nearness* (State University of New York Press, Albany, 1994), p. 129.

6 *The thing itself and its seasons*

1   A letter from José Rodrìguez Feo to Stevens, February 1952, included in *Secretaries of the Moon*, eds B. Coyle and A. Filreis (Duke University Press, Durham, N.C., 1986), p. 193.

2   'Wallace Stevens' Poetry of Being', op. cit. p. 146. I'd like to thank Josh Cohen for pointing me towards 'Nuances of a Theme by Williams'.

3   Roy Harvey Pearce, 'Wallace Stevens: Last Lesson of the Master', in *The Act of the Mind*, op. cit. pp. 121–42; and Randall Jarrell's review of the *Collected Poems* in *Yale Review*, vol. XLIV (Spring 1955), pp. 340–53, reprinted in *Wallace Stevens: The Critical Heritage*, edited by Charles Doyle (Routledge, London, 1985), pp. 411–24.

4   See Frank Kermode, *Wallace Stevens* (Faber, London, 1960), p. 32; Gardner, 'Wallace Stevens and Metaphysics', op. cit. p. 327.

5   Ibid., p. 326.

6   For a fascinating study of Stevens that analyses the 'as if', see Jacque-
    line Vaught Brogan, *Stevens and Simile: A Theory of Language* (Princeton
    University Press, Princeton, 1986).

7   Bloom, *Wallace Stevens: The Poems of our Climate*, op. cit. p. 368.

8   W.B. Yeats, *Collected Poems* (Macmillan, London, 1982), pp. 391–2.

9   In this connection, see Helen Vendler's *Wallace Stevens: Words Chosen Out
    of Desire* (University of Tennessee Press, Knoxville, 1984).

10 I'd like to thank J. Hillis Miller for bringing this poem to my
    attention.

Conclusion

1   Stevens to P. Vidal, 9 December 1953, cited by Edward Ragg in 'The
    "In-Visible" Abstract: Stevens, Coleridge and the New Critics',
    unpublished PhD chapter.

2   See 'Literature and the Right to Death', in *The Gaze of Orpheus*, trans.
    L. Davis (Station Hill, N.Y., 1981), pp. 21–62.

3   See Francis Ponge, *Le Parti pris des choses* (Gallimard, Paris, 1967).

Afterword: Calm – on Terrence Malick

1   Wittgenstein, *Culture and Value*, ed. G.H. von Wright (Blackwell,
    Oxford, 1980), p. 80.

2   Hodder & Stoughton, London, 1998.

3   Hodder & Stoughton, London, 1998.

4   Cited in Jimmie E. Cain, Jr '"Writing in his Musical Key": Terrence
    Malick's Vision of *The Thin Red Line*', *Film Criticism*, vol. XXV (2000),
    pp. 2–24.

5   'On Malick's Subjects', in *Senses of Cinema*, www.sensesofcinema.com,
    2000.

6 Martin Heidegger, *The Essence of Reasons*, trans. T. Malick, North-western University Press, Evanston, 1969.

7 For a similar line of argument on the relation of philosophy to film, see Stephen Mulhall, *On Film* (Routledge, London, 2002).

8 What is particularly intriguing is that the passages quoted above are lifted from a speech by Prewitt in *From Here to Eternity*. Jones writes,

> It was hard to accept that he, who was the hub of this known universe, would cease to exist, but it was an inevitability and he did not shun it. He only hoped that he would meet it with the same magnificent indifference with which she who had been his mother met it. Because it was there, he felt, that the immortality he had not seen was hidden (op. cit. p. 28).

The question is why Malick replaces 'magnificent indifference' with 'calm'. This passage was brought to my attention by Cain's 'Writing in his Musical Key', op. cit. p. 6.

9 Heidegger, 'What is Metaphysics?', in *Martin Heidegger: Basic Writings*, ed. D.F. Krell (Routledge, London and New York, 1978), p. 102.

10 'A Feeling of Extraordinary Lightness, a Sort of Beatitude', Blanchot, *L'instant de ma mort* (Fata Morgana, Montpellier, 1994).

11 Wittgenstein, *Tractatus Logico-Philosophicus*, trans. D.F. Pears and B.F. McGuiness (Routledge, London and New York, 1961), 6.4311.

Thanks

1 'The Philosophical Significance of a Poem', *Proceedings of the Aristotelian Society*, vol. XCVI (1995–6), pp. 269–91. Reprinted in the revised edition of *Very Little . . . Almost Nothing* (Routledge, London and New York, 2004), pp. 215–36.

Bibliography

Works by Wallace Stevens

Collected Poems (Knopf, New York, 1955/Faber, London, 1955).

The Necessary Angel: Essays on Reality and the Imagination (Knopf, New York, 1951/Faber, London, 1960).

The Palm at the End of the Mind, edited by Holly Stevens (Vintage, New York, 1967).

Opus Posthumous, revised, enlarged and corrected edition, edited by Milton J. Bates (Knopf, New York, 1989/Faber, London, 1990).

Letters of Wallace Stevens, edited by Holly Stevens (Knopf, New York, 1966).

Secretaries of the Moon: The Letters of Wallace Stevens and José Rodrìguez Feo, eds Beverly Coyle and Alan Filreis (Duke University Press, Durham, N.C., 1986).

Works on Wallace Stevens

Altieri, Charles, 'Stevens's Ideas of Feeling: Towards an Exponential Poetics', *Centennial Review,* 36 (1992), pp. 139–74.

Baird, James, *The Dome and the Rock: Structure in the Poetry of Wallace Stevens* (Johns Hopkins University Press, Baltimore, Md., 1968).

Bates, Milton J., *Wallace Stevens: A Mythology of Self* (University of California Press, Berkeley, 1985).

Berger, Charles, *Forms of Farewell: The Late Poetry of Wallace Stevens* (University of Wisconsin Press, Madison, 1985).

Bevis, W., *Mind of Winter: Wallace Stevens, Meditation and Literature* (University of Pittsburgh Press, Pittsburgh, Pa., 1988).

Bloom, Harold, *Wallace Stevens: The Poems of Our Climate* (Cornell University Press, Ithaca, N.Y., 1976).

Bove, Paul A., *Destructive Poetics: Heidegger and Modern American Poetry* (Columbia University Press, New York, 1980).

Brogan, Jacqueline V., *Stevens and Simile: A Theory of Language* (Princeton University Press, Princeton, N.J., 1986).

Bruns, Gerald, 'Stevens Without Epistemology', in Albert Gelpi, *Wallace Stevens: The Poetics of Modernism* (Cambridge University Press, Cambridge, 1985), pp. 24–40.

Byers, T.B., *What I Cannot Say: Self, Word, and World in Whitman, Stevens and Merwin* (University of Illinois Press, Urbana, 1989).

Cleghorn, Angus L., *Wallace Stevens's Poetics: The Neglected Rhetoric* (Palgrave, London, 2000).

Cook, Eleanor, *Poetry, Word-Play and Word-War in Wallace Stevens* (Princeton University Press, Princeton, N.J., 1988).

Doggett, Frank, *Stevens' Poetry of Thought* (Johns Hopkins University Press, Baltimore, Md., 1966).

Doggett, Frank and Buttel, Robert, *Wallace Stevens: A Celebration* (Princeton University Press, Princeton, N.J., 1980).

Doyle, Charles, *Wallace Stevens: The Critical Heritage* (Routledge, London and New York, 1985).

Filreis, A., *Wallace Stevens and the Actual World* (Princeton University Press, Princeton, N.J., 1991).

Filreis, A., *Modernism from Right to Left: Wallace Stevens, the 1930s and Literary Radicalism* (Cambridge University Press, Cambridge, 1994).

bibliography

Fisher, Barbara M., *Wallace Stevens: The Intensest Rendezvous* (University Press of Virginia, Charlottesville, 1990).

Fuchs, Daniel, *The Comic Spirit of Wallace Stevens* (Duke University Press, Durham, N.C., 1963).

Gardner, Sebastian, 'Wallace Stevens and Metaphysics: The Plain Sense of Things', *European Journal of Philosophy*, 2: 3 (1994), pp. 322–44.

Gelpi, Albert, *Wallace Stevens: The Poetics of Modernism* (Cambridge University Press, Cambridge, 1985), pp. 24–40.

Grey, Thomas C., *The Wallace Stevens Case: Law and the Practice of Poetry* (Harvard University Press, Cambridge, Mass., 1991).

Hertz, David Michael, *Emersonian Unfoldings in Wright, Stevens, and Ives* (Southern Illinois University Press, Carbondale, 1993).

Hillis Miller, J., *Poets of Reality: Six Twentieth-Century Writers* (Harvard University Press, Cambridge, Mass., 1965).

Hillis Miller, J., *Topographies* (Stanford University Press, Stanford, Calif., 1995).

Hillis Miller, J., *On Literature* (Routledge, London and New York, 2002).

Hines, T., *The Later Poetry of Wallace Stevens: Phenomenological Parallels with Husserl and Heidegger* (Bucknell University Press, Lewisburg, Va., 1976).

Hollander, John, 'The Sound of the Music of Music and Sound', in Frank Doggett and Robert Buttel, *Wallace Stevens: A Celebration* (Princeton University Press, Princeton, N.J., 1980), pp. 235–55.

Jenkins, L.M., *Wallace Stevens: Rage for Order* (University of Sussex Press, Brighton, 2000).

Kermode, Frank, *Wallace Stevens* (Faber, London, 1960).

La Guardia, David M., *Advance on Chaos: The Sanctifying Imagination of Wallace Stevens* (Brown University Press, Hanover, N.H., 1983).

Lakritz, A.M., *Modernism and the Other in Stevens, Frost and Moore* (University Press of Florida, Gainesville, 1996).

Leggett, B.J., *Wallace Stevens and Poetic Theory: Conceiving the Supreme Fiction* (University of North Carolina Press, Chapel Hill, 1987).

Leggett, B.J., *Early Stevens: The Nietzschean Intertext* (Duke University Press, Durham, N.C., 1992).

Lensing, G.S., *Wallace Stevens and the Seasons* (Louisiana State University Press, Baton Rouge, 2001).

Lentricchia, Frank, *The Gaiety of Language: An Essay on the Radical Poetics of W.B. Yeats and Wallace Stevens* (University of California Press, Berkeley, 1968).

Lentricchia, Frank, *Modernist Quartet* (Duke University Press, Durham, N.C., 1994).

Leonard, J.S., *The Fluent Mundo: Wallace Stevens and the Structure of Reality* (University of Georgia Press, Athens, 1988).

Levin, Jonathan, *Wallace Stevens and the Pragmatist Imagination: Towards a Literary Ecology, the Literature of Place* (Institut für Litteraturhistore, Aarhus, 1998).

Litz, A. Walton, *Introspective Voyager: The Poetic Development of Wallace Stevens* (Oxford University Press, New York, 1972).

Longenbach, J., *Wallace Stevens: The Plain Sense of Things* (Oxford University Press, New York, 1991).

Maeder, Beverly, *Wallace Stevens's Experimental Language: The Lion in the Lute* (Macmillan, Basingstoke, 1999).

McCann, Janet, *Wallace Stevens Revisited: 'The Celestial Possible'* (Prentice Hall, London, 1995).

McMahon, William E., *The Higher Humanism of Wallace Stevens* (E. Mellen Press, Lewiston, Pa., 1990).

Murphy, Charles M., *Wallace Stevens: A Spiritual Poet in a Secular Age* (Paulist Press, New York, 1997).

Pearce, R.H., 'Towards Decreation: Stevens and the Theory of Poetry', in Frank Doggett and Robert Buttel, *Wallace Stevens: A Celebration* (Princeton University Press, Princeton, N.J., 1980).

Pearce, R.H. and Hillis Miller, J., *The Act of the Mind: Essays on the Poetry of Wallace Stevens* (Johns Hopkins University Press, Baltimore, Md., 1965).

bibliography

Ragg, Edward, 'The "In-Visible" Abstract: Stevens, Coleridge and the New Critics', unpublished PhD chapter, University of Cambridge.

Riddel, Joseph, *The Clairvoyant Eye: The Poetry and Poetics of Wallace Stevens* (Louisiana State University Press, Baton Rouge, 1967).

Rieke, A., *The Sense of Nonsense*, (University of Iowa Press, Iowa City, 1992).

Sampson, Theodore, *A Cure of the Mind: The Poetics of Wallace Stevens* (Black Rose Books, Montreal and New York, 2000).

Schwarz, Daniel R., *Narrative and Representation in the Poetry of Wallace Stevens* (St Martin's Press, New York, 1993).

Serio, J.N., *Wallace Stevens: An Annotated Secondary Bibliography* (University of Pittsburgh Press, Pittsburgh, Pa., 1994).

Sharp, Tony, *Wallace Stevens: A Literary Life* (St Martin's Press, New York, 2000).

Sukenick, Ronald, *Wallace Stevens: Musing the Obscure* (New York University Press, New York, 1967).

Vendler, Helen, 'The Qualified Assertions of Wallace Stevens', in *The Act of the Mind: Essays on the Poetry of Wallace Stevens*, edited by R.H. Pearce and J. Hillis Miller (Johns Hopkins University Press, Baltimore, Md., 1965), pp. 143–65.

Vendler, Helen, *On Extended Wings: Wallace Stevens' Longer Poems* (Harvard University Press, Cambridge, Mass., 1969).

Vendler, Helen, *Wallace Stevens. Words Chosen out of Desire* (University of Tennessee Press, Knoxville, 1984).

Ziarek, Krysztof, *Inflected Language: Toward a Hermeneutic of Nearness* (State University of New York Press, Albany, 1994).

Other works consulted

Adorno, T.W., *Negative Dialektik* (Suhrkamp, Frankfurt am Main, 1966), p. 364.

Bishop, Elizabeth, *Complete Poems* (Chatto and Windus, London, 1991).

Blanchot, Maurice, *The Gaze of Orpheus* (Station Hill, N.Y., 1981).

Blanchot, Maurice, *L'instant de ma mort* (Fata Morgana, Montpellier, 1994).

Cain, Jimmie E. Jr, '"Writing in his Musical Key": Terrence Malick's Vision of *The Thin Red Line*', *Film Criticism*, vol. XXV (2000), pp. 2–24.

Coleridge, S.T., *Biographia Literaria*, ed. George Watson (Dent, London, 1965).

Coleridge, S.T., *Poems*, ed. John Beer (Dent, London, 1974).

Emerson, R.W., *Selected Essays*, ed. L. Ziff (Penguin, London, 1982).

Filippidis, Michael, 'On Malick's Subjects', in *Senses of Cinema*, www.sensesofcinema.com, 2000.

Fodor, Jerry *The Mind Doesn't Work That Way* (MIT Press, Cambridge, Mass., 2001).

Geuss, Raymond, 'Poetry and Knowledge', *Arion*, II: i (spring/summer 2003), pp. 1–31.

Hegel, G.W.F., *Introductory Lectures on Aesthetics*, trans. B. Bosanquet (Penguin, Harmondsworth, 1993).

Heidegger, M., *Being and Time*, trans. J. Macquarrie and E. Robinson (Blackwell, Oxford, 1962).

Heidegger, M., *The Essence of Reasons*, trans. T. Malick (Northwestern University Press, Evanston, Ill., 1969).

Heidegger, M., *Basic Writings*, ed. D.F. Krell (Routledge, London and New York, 1978).

Hockney, David, *The Blue Guitar* (Petersburg Press, London and New York, 1977).

Hölderlin, Friedrich, *Poems and Fragments*, trans. M. Hamburger (Cambridge University Press, Cambridge, 1980).

Jones, James, *From Here to Eternity* (Hodder & Stoughton, London, 1998).

Jones, James, *The Thin Red Line* (Hodder & Stoughton, London, 1998).

Kant, I., *Critique of Pure Reason*, trans. N. Kemp Smith (Macmillan, London, 1983).

bibliography

Livingstone, Angela, *Poems from Chevengur* (Gililand Press, Clacton-on-Sea, 2004).

Merleau-Ponty, Maurice, *Phenomenology of Perception*, trans. Colin Smith (Routledge, London, 1962).

Mulhall, Stephen, *On Film* (Routledge, London, 2002).

Ponge, Francis, *Le Parti pris des choses* (Gallimard, Paris, 1967).

Putnam, Hilary, *Realism with a Human Face* (Harvard University Press, Cambridge, Mass., 1990).

Schlegel, Friedrich, *Philosophical Fragments*, trans. Peter Firchow (University of Minnesota Press, Minneapolis, 1991).

Taylor, Charles, 'Overcoming Epistemology' in *After Philosophy: End or Transformation?* eds K. Baynes, J. Bohman and T. McCarthy (MIT Press, Cambridge, Mass., 1987).

Wittgenstein, Ludwig, *Tractatus Logico-Philosophicus*, trans. D.F. Pears and B.F. McGuiness (Routledge, London and New York, 1961).

Wittgenstein, Ludwig, *Culture and Value*, ed. G.H. von Wright (Blackwell, Oxford, 1980).

Yeats, W.B., *Collected Poems* (Macmillan, London, 1982).

Index